Restored

A JOURNEY FROM ABUSE TO DELIVERANCE

SANDRIAN NELSON-MOON

Restored

SANDRIAN NELSON-MOON

Dedication

To my son and daughter, you saved my life!

Restored

Copyright © 2022

Restored: A Journey from Abuse to Deliverance by Sandrian Nelson-Moon

All rights reserved.

All rights reserved. No parts of this publication may be reproduced, stored in a retrieval system, or transmitted in any form or by any means—for example, electronic, photocopy, recording—without the prior written permissions of the author and/or publisher. The only exception is brief quotations in printed reviews.

At times, graphic in nature, this book recounts certain events in the life of Sandrian Nelson-Moon according to her recollection and perspective. In addition to some graphic instances in the lives of various public figures and community leaders. The purpose of this book is not to defame, but to empower and motivate readers to face their challenges while equipping readers with knowledge and practical strategies to persist.

SANDRIAN NELSON-MOON

Contents

INTRODUCTION 7

Section 1: **THE ELEMENTS** 15

Section 2: **THE EXPERIENCES** 49

Section 3: **THE EFFECTS** 105

Section 4: **THE ELEVATION** 151

Section 5: **THE EXPANSION** 173

Restored

SANDRIAN NELSON-MOON

Introduction

A recent National Survey of Children's Health found that almost 50 percent of children in the United States have had at least one significant traumatic experience. Even more recently, a study from 2019 by the U.S Centers for Disease Control and Prevention (CDC) found that 60 percent of American adults report having had at least one adverse childhood experience (ACE). And almost a quarter reported three or more ACEs. These numbers are even more sobering when you consider that the CDC researchers believe the to be an underestimate.

Sexual violence happens more frequently than we want to admit or discuss. Many survivors choose to keep their trauma a deeply buried secret, an experience hidden and protected under lock and key. They spend their lives suffering in the silence of shame. I, however, will not condone a world where the victimized are voiceless. No longer will I, or any other woman who has experienced this pain, feel forced to suffer in silence.

Restored

This entire book project challenges the cultural phenomenon of secret sexual abuse.

But before those of us who have lived through this can confront and change the world, we must first confront and change ourselves. The process of healing from sexual trauma is far from easy—in fact, it is the most difficult journey that a person can embark upon. Despite what we've been told, sexual abuse is not a normal part of life, and not something that those who have suffered with and from it can simply get over. There is nothing normal about having your innocence and ability to trust snatched from you. There is nothing normal about having your sexuality perverted. There is nothing normal about having your self-worth and sense of physical and emotional safety shattered. These aren't experiences that you can just get over.

But you can heal. You can have the life that God destined for you.

You can be restored. It takes time, work, and prayer. And it certainly takes bravery to uncover what you've hidden and ran from for years.

This work of excavating hidden secrets, relieving physical and emotional trauma, and learning to love, trust, and live fully again is far from easy. Confronting your own personal truths is risky business. The truth isn't always pretty. In an age of social media culture, it's easy to always put only the prettiest glimpses of our lives forward. We've become a culture of people subconsciously trained to always put our best out front. We aim to present perfection. We hide anything that hurts. When we bear our truths for the world to see, we run the risk of being judged. Questioned. Shamed. Not only by people that we don't know, but by those we do. So, we hide instead. But I am here as living proof that you cannot heal in hiding.

Restored

As you will see in my story, I had a fairly happy childhood, but there were certain points of my life that were brutal.

Being sexually violated several times changed me forever. Nevertheless, I want you to know that this is not a "woe is me" project. I am resilient. I have endurance. I am a survivor. And you are too.

Throughout this book, I speak candidly about the impact of childhood sexual abuse in my own life. Although there are a plethora of books on the subject matter, I wanted to add a more honest look at the challenges that survivors face. With this project, I want you to understand that pain is never easy; it is never expected and often avoided. It never checks its victim's preparedness. It happens instantly and demands adjustment. Pain happens and will continue to happen.

That is inevitable and, for the most part, out of our control. What is within our control is our response.

Healing is a choice. It is intentional. And, if you take anything away from this book, I want you to know that it is possible.

The journey of healing is a process. It can be painful and transformative, all in the same breath. Healing is where we grow. It feeds our ability to expand and become stronger. Even when we are required to revisit our pain on this journey, the experiences that hurt us the most can trigger the most amazing outcomes. Healing is where we change, and change, while hard, is incredibly beautiful. Many of us fear change because of the possibility of pain that can come with it, and the new uncertainties and unexplainable (feelings) that change often brings.

But we don't realize that the unexplainable can open the door for the unimaginable. Unimaginable joy. Unimaginable love. An unimaginable life.

Restored

My hope with this book is to help you see the unimaginable possibilities that every encounter your life brings, even the most painful ones can make way for amazing things. During my abuse, and in the years that followed, I couldn't have imagined that my pain and hurt would have led me to the woman I am now. I have been blessed with my two beautiful children, Makaela, 13, and my wonderful 8-year-old son Mnason. I have an amazing husband Walter, and his boys- my two older sons, Jalen and Jaquan, my fabulous parents Marcia and Clovis Sr., my brother Clovis Jr., my great sisters Petagaye, Alyssa, Katherine and Veronique, friends: Fiona, Adron,Tamara, Nadine, Alicia, Georgia, and Alexia. I also have an amazing mixed family that supports me. In addition to people, I have purpose.

I believe I am a change agent, and my God-given assignment is to help transcend others in their own journey to a fulfillment of self and purpose.

Perhaps, like me, your story is meant to be shared to help others. You may or may not feel that desire stirring in your spirit. If you do, I hope that you will follow that path. But first, you must allow yourself to experience that story again, and, this time, experience it with the understanding that it happened for a very specific reason. All pain has purpose.

I share some intense moments throughout this book, moments that may remind you of your own experiences, or those of someone you know. If you are someone who has suffered from sexual abuse, I hope that you will read my story not simply to relive pain, but to learn how to live through it.

As you move through each chapter, I pray that your courage builds. I pray that you feel a growing desire to take my story and begin to uncover your own.

Restored

Take the time to do the *Life Application* and *Restoration Exploration* work at the end of each chapter, as those exercises were created to guide your reflections and propel you forward.

You can do this.

You will do this. You can be restored.

Let's begin your journey from abuse to deliverance.

Section 1

The Elements
Growing up Jamaican

Kingston. Jamaica. With its exotic beaches and jaw-dropping waterfalls, the place where I was born is one of the most sought-after vacation spots in the world. Known as the birthplace of reggae music, Jamaican rum, Bob Marley, and the cradle of some of the world's greatest athletes, Jamaica is so much more to me. It was the first place where I learned love. The first place where I tasted freedom. The first place that I called home.

Restored

Whenever I think about Jamaica, two words come to mind: home and food. People were a significant part of both.

Some of the best parts of my childhood were spent running barefoot through the yard, feeding animals on the farm where I was raised and climbing from tree to tree like a monkey. I loved riding on my grandfather's donkey cart with him and spending every hour I could outside with my cousins. During the holidays Jamaica came alive with traditions and practices. Christmas especially was an adventure. We would whitewash stones using a powder and water concoction my grandmother would mix for us. After we painted the stones, we would place them around the plants in the front yard. We would spend time preparing our home with precision. We baked, we changed everything from curtains to sheets. We decorated our tree and yard with lights, ordered special cuts of meat and rearranged the furniture.

It was something we looked forward to every year. In fact, every Christmas after we had dinner, and cleaned up, my cousins and I would get dressed and go out to *Half-Way Tree*. We'd take pictures and get ice cream. There were hundreds of people there too, hanging out and celebrating. It was one of the many magical places on the island. Outside of our traditional holiday celebrations, Jamaicans had parties all the time. During the week before and after school, the buses and cab cars were filled with music and activities. We had parties on our block regularly. Everyone in the neighborhood knew each other, so that sense of family and love were always in the air.

Some parties would happen on my block. Some adults were serious about creating a perfect atmosphere. They would place bags over the streetlights to darken the entire block and crank up the music into the wee hours of the morning.

Restored

They partied and danced most weekends. The children played outside a lot after school and more on weekends. We played marbles, baseball, soccer, and Chinese hopscotch with rubber bands coiled around our ankles most days we loved outside and made-up loads of games. There was no celebration of any kind in Jamaica without food. It was a consistent thing to cook and bring food.

I've traveled tons of places, but the earthy, organic taste of food in Jamaica is second to none. Even the fast-food restaurants are a totally different experience than in the United States. But while the juicy chicken served at McDonald's and KFC were unlike anything you'd ever taste, none of it could hold a candle to the legendary, home cooked food that you could find on almost any street corner in Kingston. A Jamaican can take the simplest ingredients and turn them into amazing meals. We can eat corned beef and rice and be completely happy.

But when a Jamaican cooks, I mean *really* cook. You can taste the love and legacy in every bite.

There were "higglers", or street vendors, everywhere selling amazing, flavorful food. On Friday nights, we would go around the block for jerk chicken and jerk pork. One guy in our neighborhood sold his food out of a bodacious drum-pan. On Saturdays, the aroma of another higgler's peanut porridge would bring loads of people with their empty basins or containers, to his corner to be filled with the sweet porridge. Ms. Marcia made my favorite food. She sold it at my primary school, and she made curry chicken. She would put it in this huge pot and cook it until the meat fell from the bones. The gravy was made with perfection. Ms. Marcia would put her sticky rice into a white portable box folded on the edges and top it with her curry chicken and gravy. That first bite would leave me speechless every time.

Restored

More than thirty years later, I've never tasted anything that's even remotely comparable. Her food was ridiculously good.

Jamaicans took pride in making sure that food was always available and that no one around them was ever hungry.

From Ms. Marcia's curry chicken that felt like a feast, to the rice, fried egg, and dumplings with butter that my grandmother would roast over wood chips to make a meager meal that fed a house full of people, to the boats we run (a Jamaican term for cooking outdoors), food brought and kept us together. It was at the center of every celebration, big or small. It didn't have to be much at all, but it was always enough. That is the heart of Jamaica that I've always known.

Yet, Jamaica will always be a place of beauty, strength, and sorrow. It is amazing how somewhere that you love so much and holds so many happy memories could cause you so much pain.

SANDRIAN NELSON-MOON

I know I am not the only girl child who grew up there who felt the same. Born in one of the poorest hospitals in the world, my childhood unfolded in a gang-infested neighborhood where robberies were rampant, and mayhem was everywhere I turned. The violence happened so frequently, that it became a part of our everyday lives. Gangs ran the streets. Thieves ran through backyards, chased by the cops. Men spent their days posted on concrete blocks in front of their small homes and ran drug rings. Gunmen shot up homes. Murders happened when you least expected it, day, and night. Even some of the police worked for the local gangs. It was nothing to watch officers dump dead bodies in the back of their trucks. When you can't trust the very people who are paid to protect you, there was a part of you that felt that no one could cover you. In the world, your life meant little.

Home was—or at least should be—the one place a child should be safe.

Restored

Like most ghettos, the crime rates were high, but so was the love. We were a community simply struggling to survive. On both sides of Malverne Avenue, the street I grew up on, were families who'd lived in that neighborhood for generations. Regardless of what went on around us, there was a sense of good that bonded us. In Kingston, crime wasn't always a choice. Of course, there were people who could care less about any lives other than their own. But there were many who saw crime as a way out—a passport out of the pain of poverty. Despite all the despair around us, the other children that I knew found some way to remain happy and hopeful. There was a joy in us that nothing or nobody could completely take away. We ran. We played. We dreamed. Those were the things that the violence we were surrounded by couldn't rob us of and that we didn't need money to buy.

As a little girl, you can't miss what you've never had. I never looked around and counted what I didn't have.

That's the beauty of home: the culture was so rich that I never once realized we were poor. Yes, we didn't have much financially, I had my version of family around me. We were disjointed at times, but I always knew what home was.

My mother is of Cuban-Jamaican descent. My grandfather, his mom and his twin sister escaped Castro's rule at a young age, migrated to Jamaica, and eventually met my grandmother who hailed from St. Mary in the hills of the island. My mother, a fraternal twin, was one of their nine children. While our family had my grandfather's Latin blood in our veins, Jamaica was, and always would be, who we were. I knew nothing but Jamaica and its culture. Jamaica was my everything.

I could trace my mother's roots back for generations, but I never knew much about my father's family.

I was about two years old when my mother and father went their separate ways.

Restored

He moved just outside of Kingston, and he would come to see my brother and me as often as possible, first by himself, and then years later, with his new wife. I'll be honest, at first, it was weird for me to see him with her and eventually with the daughters that they'd have together. I grew to accept his new family as my own, but at times I felt more distant from my dad than any daughter should. I didn't know it then, but I needed more of his protection and presence. As my mom worked hard and long hours to make a better life for my siblings and I, later I realized what mom's plan to stabilize things financially would mean.

My grandparents allowed my brother, sister, and me to live with them, alongside my other 7 cousins who were close to our ages. My grandparents were strict but cared for us greatly.

My grandmother and grandfather each took responsibility for teaching and guiding us on the things that, while I couldn't appreciate them then, I certainly would. Neither of them sat us down and explained what they were doing, but, like most parents, they believed their primary job was to pass down the knowledge and practical skills they knew we needed to survive in this world. The Caribbean way was to prepare their children for life. For my grandma, it was preparing the girls to take care of home. Among other things, it was important for her that we knew how to wash, cook, and clean. We'd start cleaning early Saturday morning before everyone else was up and, by noon, the house was spic-and-span clean.

My grandfather worked hard his entire life and taught us to do the same. We lived in the city, but we had a farm in our own backyard.

We had a plethora of goats, pigs, cows, etc.

Restored

I grew up getting fresh eggs from a chicken's butt with no disgust or fear. I could single handedly kill, remove feathers, and cut a chicken in the joints like a butcher, without hesitation. We had a donkey in the back that my grandfather would hitch a cart to and let me ride with him to cut grass for the cows. Even with his strictness, my grandfather made time for play. Hide and seek with him were hallmarks of my childhood, although I got caught every time. I could never sit still long enough to let my grandfather find me. I spent many-a-day running around the backyard barefoot with cousins, frolicking through the bushes, and working the farm. That was joy for me.

In his own way, my grandfather taught us that the load could be heavy and light.

That, even in small ways, there could and should be work and play. That little money in no way meant less life.

When we weren't in school or helping our grandparents, to keep myself occupied during the day, I'd play school with my cousins. I'd be the teacher. There were white pieces of drywall that fell from the ceiling in the backroom of our house. I would collect them and use them for chalk. My chalkboard was the zinc fence outside in our yard that separated our house and the neighbors. When my cousins didn't want to be my students, I'd line up stones like attentive children and make them into my classroom. If I wasn't teaching, I was counseling clients at my imaginary law firm. There was something in me that always wanted to support, teach, and protect others. It's no surprise that I loved being in school.

Early School Days.

I went to 2 preschools and 2 elementary schools. The first elementary school was a catholic school. I met my best friend there.

Restored

I was then sent to Pembroke Hall Primary after almost everyone in our family had attended there before me. All the teachers knew my family and they welcomed me with open arms. I was a super skinny kid who was pretty reserved, and always managed to make friends. My mom told me that whenever she would drop me off, I often went off by myself, but by the end of the day, I would greet her again after school with at least five new friends. Between the adults and being surrounded by the kids in my neighborhood that I already knew, school made me feel safe.

I always saw school as a place where children could explore the things that they really loved.

One of the beauties of school in the Caribbean was that we all wore uniforms, so we didn't spend much time competing with shoes and clothes.

Money mattered in other ways at times, like when, some days, I didn't have the money to buy a school lunch and would have to hurry home to eat and race back to school. But for the most part, in school, we were equals. If anything, we were separated more by academics and special interests than socioeconomic status.

My dad was really serious about our education. Though I loved school and would have done my best, anyway, making good grades was a big deal for him. We were well-behaved children, so we didn't need to be disciplined to do what we were supposed to do, but my father incentivized us to stay on track with the prize he knew we held dear—gifts and money. For Christmas, our reward for getting good grades was shopping. He'd take us to the store and let us pick whatever we wanted. We'd be in heaven.

Restored

One year, we each got BMX bikes, and were the talk of the neighborhood. When my mother moved to the states, she would send me $5 US dollars. $1 US dollar was almost $100 in Jamaican currency at the time, which was a lot to me when I initially got the bill in the mailbox. She could have sent me enough to buy some banana chips and a juice box, and I would have been elated. But once I found out how far that $5 could stretch, in my mind, that small amount made me rich. Whether it was money from my father or my mother, I knew that when I got good grades, I would be rewarded for it.

School wasn't just about the books. For a lot of kids, it was our dream space, a place where we could discover talents and gifts that most of us didn't know we had. There was sports and the arts.

With a part of our school's lot set aside for track and field, students took the sport seriously. Some of my friends would train day and night.

A true tomboy, I enjoyed physical education too, but I came alive when it was time to perform. I was a shy girl, but there was something about a stage that lit me up. At school, we'd open our songbooks/hymnals to set the tone for the day. I would sing my heart out. I sang like an angel, and it is a gift that both my brother and I inherited from my father's side of the family. My dad's sister, Aunt Grace, was musically inclined. Although I only met her once, maybe twice, before she was murdered.

I would hear stories of how beautiful her voice was, and how she would have taken the music industry by storm had her life not been stolen from her. And although dad was an educator and businessman, he was a great singer as well.

Like Aunt Grace, he spent some time in the studio recording music. Singing was as natural to us as breathing. Needless to say, my favorite part of school was the choir.

Restored

Even knowing that I could sing well and had actually performed in front of my family since I was three years old, I was afraid to try out for the first time. Still, something inside of me still pushed me to come to the classroom after school for the audition. The choir teacher, Ms. Portios, stood in front of the group and guided us through a series of songs. As we sang, she walked toward me. The rest of the students got quiet as she got closer. I wanted to sink into the floor. I was prepared for her to tell me that I sounded horrible, compared to some of the other girls.

As I braced myself for her criticism, and the humiliation that would be sure to follow, I nervously stood still. "I can hear the voice in you," she said, looking me right in the eye. "You just need to open your mouth."

She placed her hands on my stomach and quietly asked me to sing. My voice was released. That day, I sang in the highest, purest way possible, with a voice that I'd never heard before.

Mrs. Portios ignited what had laid dormant for years. At that moment, a songstress was born. A girl who felt powerful and special because she had an ability to do something that many others could not do. Unleashed, I sang everywhere. I would climb the ackee and cherry trees in the back yard and sing. I would run up to the rooftop, and just let my voice float over the neighborhood roofs.

I didn't need a microphone or a stage. Performing made me happy. I just wanted to keep feeling the joy that singing would always bring. My brother and I would go on to be diehard choral members at our school.

We even competed in various competitions across the island and won all sorts of gold medals and awards. We both had lead roles in some songs we did with the choir, and between the two of us, we sang and performed in every play and skit our school had.

Restored

Singing became our lives, and, outside of getting good grades, there was nothing more important.

In the 5th grade, my brother and I got the opportunity of a lifetime—our choir was asked to perform live on a local television station, JBCTV. The idea of being seen on camera all over the island was the most exciting thing that had ever happened to us. We were ecstatic. Our teacher didn't have to tell us how huge this was. We were just about at the end of the school year, and there were exams to worry about on top of preparing to perform. It didn't matter. The extra practices were worth it. We were on cloud nine.

The week we were set to make our television debut, our mother came to us with some news.

She'd decided to fly to the United States. She told my brother and I that she was going there to work, which didn't surprise us.

We knew that she was doing everything she could to create a good life for our family, including getting a house of our own where we could all be together. We were sad to see her go, but we believed that it wouldn't be for long. But her leaving us wasn't the worst part of what she had to share.

She was leaving on the same day as our television performance. I knew she really wanted my brother and me to see her off. I didn't know it then, but she wasn't going to America for a quick stay. She was migrating there and would never come back to Jamaica to live permanently again.

Maybe I should have been more torn about not going to the airport, but my little-girl mind couldn't see beyond what I wanted at that moment, and that was to perform with my choir on television. I knew I would see my mother again soon. But being on television was a once-in-a-lifetime opportunity.

Restored

Our world revolved around music and performing at that time, and I loved it so much. There was no way that I was going to miss any chance to sing, especially this one.

My family packed up to take mom to the airport. I could see the hurt in my mother's eyes when she realized her kids weren't going.

The choir performance was my priority that day. I gave mom a hug and kiss and ran to prepare for my time to shine.

Once we arrived at the studio, I was in literal bliss. I remember coming home with my brother and being ecstatic about everything that we'd seen. From walking in the sound stage, meeting the camera crew, and seeing the red "Live on TV" ignite, I was living the dream of a superstar. I thought about my mom a lot that day. I hoped she'd made it safely.

I knew she'd write to me, and as I thought about what I'd say in my letter back, I couldn't wait to tell her all about being in the studio.

I sang for years, but that studio experience wasn't nearly as life defining as my mother's departure was. We were used to living with our grandparents and always had a sense of family there with them.

 Our uncle and cousins were in the same house with us, now with my mother out of the country and my father with his new family, it would mean that there was nowhere else for us to go if we ever needed to.

With my grandparents, I was in good hands. It was never a day I went without a meal, or clothes, or shoes. What I missed was the love and protection that children should feel from their parents.

My mom called and she would write me letters, so we stayed in touch. But there was nothing like having her or my father with me, and for them to see me the way that I needed to be seen.

Restored

Sometimes I felt that my grandmother treated us differently. My grandparents took good care of my physical needs. However, my soul still suffered for so many reasons. I felt that nobody ever truly saw *me*.

The world looked at me and through me, but never stopped to see that quiet, shy, isolated little girl who needed more. The one who felt lost, lonely, and when she wasn't singing, wasn't sure if her voice was heard or mattered to anyone. The one who was hiding in plain sight.

The one who was just smiling and pretending that everything was always okay, even when it wasn't. Being unseen was just the beginning of my personal pain that nobody ever knew, at least until now.

Hiding our hurt is not something that we're born to do. If you've ever been a mother or spent any time with a baby, you know that, from birth, they instinctually cry out when they are in need.

It isn't until adults begin to chastise them for expressing themselves and running to people they can trust to share when they're hurt, that children begin to suppress their emotions.

They're conditioned to get over their pain, to smile through it, to shake it off. They are taught to hide what hurts—even when they're right and the world is wrong. You may be like me, and you've struggled with hiding your hurt. I started this book by sharing so much of my childhood experiences, before the sexual abuse, to prove something important to you. That is, abuse can happen to anyone at any time. When a woman is preyed upon, it can be easy for people to wonder what was wrong with her, not the predator. We are conditioned to question and judge her, as if she could have somehow caused what happened to her.

Restored

If we're talking about a child, we ask, "Did he or she come from a broken home?" or "Was he or she 'fast?'" If a woman is violated, we ask things like, "How was she dressed?", "Why was she out that late at night by herself?" or "Why did she go over there in the first place?"

Abuse wasn't *supposed* to happen to me. An innocent little girl who lived a happy life. A girl who loved school and had friends and sang and played teacher with her cousins. But it wouldn't have mattered what my background or home life was.

A child could still have their basic needs met and have a roof over their head, food to eat, and friends, and still be hurt within those walls that they called home. Abuse can happen to anyone, no matter the sex. Poor and rich. Book-smart and street smart, no matter the race or color. We're all different, except for one thing. None of us deserved what happened to us.

Abuse disrupts and interrupts life as you've always known it. And it silences you. Few people are given the space or the permission to feel what happened to them.

Instead, you're pressured to suppress your hurt, to put on a pair of emotional roller skates and move past it as quickly as possible. That, we believe, is the only way to move forward.

My family did everything they could to keep me safe and far away from the gangs and trouble that any of us could have easily fallen prey to.

So, there was this part of me that knew I needed to do the right thing. Between Christianity and family culture, not only was it a struggle to always want to do right, but to feel right. Even when I was wronged. I had to learn how to suppress to survive. And that was for all hurts, big and small.

You probably have too.

At some point in your life, you've been hurt.

Restored

I am sure that as you are reading this, realizing that you have been operating in this same mode. You've been telling yourself that this hiding and pretending was normal and necessary. You've been minimizing your pain, reducing it to something that "just" happened to you. We'll be focused on sexual trauma in this book, but maybe that experience wasn't a part of your story. But you still lived through something that hurt you deeply. Your hurt still counts. Regardless of the offense, there was still pain. If it was significant to you, that is all that matters.

This journey, this healing process, requires that we honor it all. The small and the not-so-small. Whatever it was, whoever it was that hurt you, will be acknowledged here. Not dismissed or devalued. And certainly not suppressed or silenced.

Everything that I've endured—poverty, being overlooked and ignored, teased for my full lips, verbal, mental and sexual abuse—were all experiences that I suppressed. It would be years later that I realized how all of that affected me.

I created a safe space in my head where I could go and forget all of it. Most of the time I could. Subconsciously I locked away deep parts of myself in the process. But that is a dangerous thing to do. Our childhood memories and past pain, no matter how hard we try to hide it, can haunt us.

Those hurts show up in little ways, and they keep rearing their ugly head until all that pain erupts. The damage that ensues can be harmful, to you and the people around you.

So, we must stop hiding so we can heal.

The point of this book is to help you to uproot, debunk, learn and grow from your past pain.

Restored

Whether we are talking about growing up in the poorest of neighborhoods, being made fun of for how you looked, or mental, sexual, and physical abuse, you can bring that pain up to the surface. Today, you don't have to make do. You don't have to pretend or lie to yourself or others. You've spent so much of your life denying the most painful parts of you.

But no more.

LIFE APPLICATION PRINCIPLE:

==Suppression is sometimes necessary for survival.==

This is the part (at least the first one in this book) where you give yourself grace—and plenty of it. Disconnecting from your past pain was a necessity, not a choice. We suppress it to survive. Telling ourselves that, one day, we'll get back to it. We've fought hard to not have to face the pain. To not have to break from the weight of it all. To not have to feel the hurt, the shame, the regret that, often, isn't yours to carry. Suppression is protection. We're taught to leave the past in the past. To sweep it under the rug. That is not how you have to live. You are no longer here to simply survive. You are here to *thrive.*

I want you to see the broken pieces of you that you've been barely holding together. Admit that whatever it was or is does hurt you.

Restored

What seemed small and insignificant to you wasn't. Pain is pain. Nothing, and I mean nothing, that hurt you is meaningless.

Bring it to the surface. See it. Say it. Feel it so you can start healing it.

Restoration Exploration

Think back. What are some life experiences that you often leave covered? What are you hiding deep down? How can you begin to peel back the layers of some of your pain to lessen its infection of your present life? Reflect on those parts of yourself here.

_____
_____
_____
_____
_____
_____
_____
_____
_____
_____
_____
_____
_____
_____
_____
_____
_____
_____
_____
_____

Restored

Section 2

The Experiences
Pain & Suffering

My cousin's cousin, Lisa, and I went to school together. Not only did we see each other in school, we were neighbors too. She and her mother lived directly across the street from my grandparents' home. She was cousins with my cousin. Her dad was my cousin's uncle. We saw each other practically everywhere we went.

That day was just like any other. I got up and got ready for school like normal. I remember being a little more excited than usual.

Restored

We were beginning a new lesson in class that day, and being the bookworm I was, I couldn't wait to get to class. It's interesting how memory works—on the one hand much of that day is a blur, on the other hand there are many things about that day that I will never forget.

We'd settled into our seats for the afternoon part of our day when the classroom door flew open. A man, Lisa's dad, burst into the room, and, within seconds, grabbed one of the girls in our class by the neck, drug her to the front of the classroom, and put a knife to her throat. Her name was Kiera, and I will never forget the terror in her eyes. The other students screamed loudly. It was mayhem as we ran under the tables and screamed at the top of our lungs. I'd never felt that type of fear in my life.

Everything was happening so fast that I can't remember every detail, but I remember my 9-year-old mind racing, wondering if any of us would ever see the light of day again.

After what felt like an eternity, Lisa's dad tossed Kiera aside and ran out of the room. All our screams and tears scared him off. Still panicked and deathly afraid, we poured out into the hallway as our teachers did everything, they could, to calm the chaos, despite being horrified themselves. The entire scene was like something in a *Lifetime* movie, but it was our reality that day. We later learned exactly what happened that day and how the events unfolded.

Lisa's dad had come to the school earlier that day and tried to take her from school, but her teacher, knowing of his abusive ways, refused to have her leave with him.

Restored

Earlier that day her dad, knowing that her mom would be there to pick her up from school, camped outside of one of the local bars that was just down the street from the school. When he saw her, he pounced on her, and stabbed her several times. She died right there on the street. Then he ran into the school building, threatening to kill himself on school grounds. Our classroom happened to be the first one he saw. While he held us in the classroom, word started circulating about what happened. People in the neighborhood went after him and moved in like a mob with bats, boards, and anything that could hurt him, but he hurt himself instead. When he ran out of our classroom, we didn't leave the building as we thought. He went into the boy's bathroom and killed himself. Lisa lost both of her parents that day.

I'm not sure how we managed to return to that school building following all of the madness that happened. The reality of it all just seemed surreal. And it still does.

Since the path that Lisa's mother was murdered on was the shortest and best route to school, many of us were forced to continue to walk that way to and from school. As I walked home every day in the coming months, I was afraid. I could still see remnants of the murder scene in the alley we all frequented. I could imagine Lisa's mother's body lying there, bleeding, and probably praying that she didn't die and leave her baby girl alone.

As the situation played out, I never knew that it was Lisa's dad. It was too much for my little nine-year-old mind to comprehend, but it turned out that her father had a history of violence towards her and her mom. In fact, I overheard my aunt say he lit a bed with them both on fire once.

Another time, I remembered when Lisa and I were playing outside in front of the house once, he drove by and slipped her a note.

Restored

I later learned the note was a threat to kill her and her mom. It was a promise he partly made good on that day at the school.

I felt horrible for Lisa, in a matter of hours, she was an orphan. That day was a testament to how quickly a tragedy can alter an innocent child's life forever.

Not only was Lisa's life changed, but many of us were traumatized that day. However, none of us would know the depth of her pain from tragically losing her parents. Nothing could compare to that hurt. Yet what we saw and experienced would be etched in our minds forever. The fear that we felt was – and still is – unforgettable. None of us knew how to properly process what happened. Not a soul thought to ask us how we felt or encouraged us to cry or share our fears if we wanted to. This became its own type of traumatic event for me, to this day I can't watch someone getting stabbed on tv I can still remember her death.

Like most of the trauma that I witnessed or experienced, our family left it alone. No one said anything about what happened. So, neither did I.

As vicious as Lisa's mother's murder was, it wasn't the first time that I'd been that close to violence. When you live in a third world country, you are liable to see just about anything. From watching someone run down the street with their guts hanging out (this happened to me when I was in high school), a gunman hiding in your front yard (yes, this happened to me too), random fights, or murder, you can feel as if you are always exposed to something or someone unsafe. As you can now understand, the islands can be a place of wonder, but sometimes also a place of worry. Lots of worries.

I remember standing outside on our veranda one day and my uncle's girlfriend ran up to the house screaming and yelling at him.

Restored

Before I realized what was happening, she'd stabbed him with an ice pick. I was right next to him as she did it literally.

That same uncle contracted HIV from the woman who stabbed him, and ultimately died of AIDS. The way he died was a culmination of the volatile relationship that he and his kid's mom always had. Had she hurt him again physically, sadly, it would not have been a surprise to any of us. Their relationship spiraled out of control until one of them was removed from this earth. I believe my uncle loved her immensely and no matter what she did wouldn't let her go. For her on the other hand I believe she had some mental issues and other problems that led to her demise.

When my mother told me that he was sick, she sadly talked about his illness in a normal fashion. Without giving it a second thought, she shared how much he was suffering with all these sores over his body, rapidly losing weight, and in a lot of pain.

I'd lived with this man, and he'd been an important part of my life. But I wasn't given a chance to think about how his sickness made me feel.

Whether it was a neighbor's murder, a family member's stabbing, death, or any other violent or tragic event, my family did what so many families do in Jamaica—never speak of it again and move past trauma as quickly and quietly as possible. No one acknowledged or discussed anything painful or emotional, instead choosing to pretend their feelings were under control, or that pain didn't exist. But it definitely does. As long as you feel it, it does.

I could only wish we handled pain differently in our culture. Too many things get pushed to the side and stay there. There were so many things many of us wished were different within our Jamaica but there was still a sense of protection that you felt in your neighborhood and home.

Restored

When you were surrounded by family and people who felt like family, you could let your guard down a bit. That's how I felt for a long time.

Until that changed.

My Innocence.

As I am writing this book and thinking back over my life, I realize that nine years old was such a pivotal age for me. I've talked about so much up until this point, and so much of it happened over the span of that year. That was also the year that I began really dreaming of becoming a lawyer, and, despite my youth, connected to why that career was calling me then. What I know now is that it was because of how defenseless I felt. The personal protection I experienced in my own life was limited. I was hoping, praying, at that age someone would defend me, but they didn't. So, I wanted to defend people who couldn't defend themselves. I wanted to become who I once needed.

That's who I was then. A little girl who wanted to protect people. A little girl who desperately wanted to be protected.

I had wound down for the night. The house was quiet, and I laid there on my back with my eyes gazing at the hole in my ceiling. Soon, I began to drift off and was asleep within minutes. Suddenly I was awakened by cold hands that touched places my mom told me were private. Startled, I jumped out of my sleep. The room was completely dark. I could hear the person stumble over our backpacks and shoes as they exited the room.

What was happening? And why to me?

I was shocked. I felt naked. I felt weird, a sensation that my young body and mind had never felt before. I was in shock. My young mind was confused. I was so lost, it almost felt unreal. I was now a statistic. I was touched. This was the first time I was molested.

Restored

Though the details were fuzzy, it was clearly a violation to my mind, to my body, and to my spirit. I do not remember who it was, or why it happened, but I do know how and what I felt. It was male for sure, and he completely terrified me. I was frozen and scared. Tears welled up in my eyes and I was shaking. I remember looking over to my two cousins, hoping they saw something, heard something, but they were sound asleep. I had just gone to sleep last night like every other night. My home was safe, right? Then why? I was in this one on my own. At nine, I had a huge cross to bear.

That night, I became my own security, my own protection. I slept like a ninja, as I attempted to establish what I had hoped to be a fail-proof routine to prevent that person from coming back to hurt me again. I figured he would not return to hurt me if I kept the light on and he was exposed.

I tumbled out of my bed and turned on the lamp that was a few steps away. Then I scurried back and jumped under the blanket. While everyone else slept, I laid awake for hours. I rolled my body into a ball and let the tears soak my pillow.

Like a video that I couldn't stop, I kept replaying the image of the person's silhouette in my head. *Who was that and why would they want to hurt me?*

Soon morning came the next day, and the journey of pretending began. I said nothing to my Christian grandparents who were asleep that night, steps away from my room. How could I? I didn't know who it was, I didn't know who to blame. But I knew that I needed to protect myself. I became a detective of sorts, scoping everyone around me. Who was the perpetrator?

These are people I'm always around, I thought. *Why would someone hurt me?*

For weeks, things went back to normal.

Restored

But instead of settling me, the fact that the person didn't come back confused me further. I began to wonder if I'd made a mistake and imagined the entire thing. I decided that I was okay again, that I could rest. I felt safe again.

In time, I started allowing my body to fall asleep. And like most predators, he knew that. He knew that I wouldn't be watching and waiting everyday all year, with the lamp on, as I did the first time. He pounced on me, again and again! It was like he had an alarm that would alert him that it was time to strike again.

Defenseless, his large body would arrest mine, nearly pinning me to the bed in fear. Each time I felt more defeated than the last. It was like a part of me was silently put to death each time.

I became paranoid and scared, yet I never spoke of it. I didn't think anyone would believe me anyway, so I said nothing. For me, the stain of conversations like this was felt throughout the home.

These things were never discussed. I learned quickly that anything about the "s" word was shut down and off limits in my grandparents' home.

I remember sitting in my room with my girl cousins, talking about a boy. I was telling them how much I liked him and how cute he was, and while I probably did have a little crush, for the most part, I just wanted to have fun. As I pretended to play out my puppy love and how I would kiss and hug him (mind you, this was only in my imagination), my cousins and I fell out laughing. My grandmother was walking past the room. She heard everything I said. She busted in the room, shouting, "Mi no wah hear dat!"

Grandmother barely missed anything that went on under that roof, except what was happening to me at night. She retorted, "Go read a book! What kind of grown-up conversation is that?"

Restored

My cousins froze, terrified that they would be next on her list. Stuttering, I tried to defend myself to her and assure her I was just playing.

"You are a child, stay in a child's place!" Grandmother turned our room light off and slammed that door in disgust.

We were in trouble for entertaining grown folk conversations that involved boys. So, I knew from that day on, conversations that pertained to boys, kissing, and touching would be off limits. I wouldn't dare utter a word about the forbidden acts that happened a week prior.

I tried my best to move forward. Yet, the nightly encounters continued for a few years. I didn't realize it then, but I was never the same after that first time.

The little innocent girl had died that first day. She died with the fear and shame that came with my uncertainty.

I was smart enough to attempt to protect myself by changing my sleep habits to confuse whomever it was, but my fear also made it hard to sleep. Every sound around me at night freaked me out.

For a few years, from the time I was preparing to leave the 4th grade until I was in 7th grade, the molestation persisted. Mostly touching by 2 people while I slept, Then, it stopped suddenly. These years were the weariest time of my life. I didn't know where to turn. My family provided my basic needs. I never went without clothes or food. Yet, it was my spirit and mind that was starved.

Following the molestation, I was starved of nurturing. I craved it, but it never showed up. Once I was violated, I was scared all the time.

I would create this place in my head that would provide a sense of peace, until night fell. The molestation birthed within me a sense of defeat. Prior to that I was a joyful kid. I was an incredibly happy kid.

Restored

I was a city kid that had the heart of a country girl. I was innocent. Trusting. But that was stolen from me. Though being molested repeatedly in the middle of the night was an experience I never welcomed, the most difficult part was the reaction of the adults in my life. The lack of care was cultural. It was taboo to even bring up such an issue. It wasn't a welcoming environment for open conversations. So, I suffered in silence.

My mother's twin's house became a saving grace for me. At Uncle Via's, I would escape what I felt at home. Their home was still strictly Christian, but it was fun for me.

His daughter, my cousin Rachel, and I bonded, and I enjoyed spending weekends or summers with them. Before my mom migrated to the States, it was the one place she would let me go and stay a while. I was safe there. Rachel's house and the house next door were my escapes.

Though I had never once mouthed to them that I had experienced sexual abuse, I was at peace at their homes.

Often, I thought of my mom and dad, and how much I wished they could be there for me. My mother was in New York, working hard to get me and my siblings to America with her. She sent constant letters, she called, and sent money to help raise us. By now, my dad had become a more consistent figure in my life, but he worked all over the island. At times he would be gone for weeks, so seeing him every day did not happen. He was always only a call away.

Still, that didn't replace the need in my heart for him to be a part of my day-to-day life.

When the abuse was happening, it was unimaginable to me to tell my parents about anything. I wonder now what would have happened if I had. If I'd told my dad, would he have made it stop? Would he have defended me?

Restored

Would he have rescued me and snatched me and my brother out of that house and taken us to live with him? I said nothing. I was too afraid, ashamed, and confused to admit what was happening and if I would be blamed.

As I got older, the molestation lessened. I was relieved to not be assaulted in my sleep. While my body wasn't suffering anymore, the damage to my mind was still there. At times, I would have the desire to speak, but no words could come out.

During this time, I hardly left the yard and spent loads of time alone writing in a diary I kept hidden in a hole in the ceiling. I had to find ways of entertaining and releasing my thoughts. Emotionally, I had experienced high highs and deep lows.

One minute I was fine, the next I felt my grandmother had favorites and saw me only sometimes. To think of it, I don't think she ever really knew me. I don't think anyone did, including myself.

I don't think anyone realized they merely got a version of me all those years—a fragile version at that. I simply existed in a bubble I had now created as a shield encompassed by my feelings. Back then, when you exhibited certain behaviors, people chalked it up to you "having an attitude", "being spoiled" or some other excuse that placed the blame on you rather than the people around you or your circumstances.

It was expected that whatever it was you were going through, eventually, you would get over it and bounce back. Yes, no one knew that I was being abused. I believed that if I had told someone, nothing would change. I wouldn't have been comforted or encouraged to process my pain. Instead, I would have been forced to hide it and not feel it. No one around me, particularly my grandparents, were equipped to comprehend what I was living through every day or to offer me any help.

I found out later that I was right.

Restored

During the molestation, I could tell the difference in the kind of person I was becoming. I was nervous around people and became even more shy and very reserved. I went from a girl who loved singing, performing, playing, and pretending to a girl who would barely open her mouth to talk to anyone. I was perceived as standoffish, but I was painfully introverted.

Not knowing who to trust, I felt unsafe. There was also the shame that I carried on my shoulders like a thousand-pound weight. As badly as I wanted to be seen, I was afraid to allow anyone close to me for fear that they would look right through me and discover the dirty secret that I carried. I grew into something else and created someone else. I didn't want to seem weak to people. So, I created a totally different persona. At times, I felt like I was 2-3 different people contingent upon the situation. I was a little weird and very sensitive, yet I maintained a hard exterior.

During high school in Jamaica, I went to Merl Grove High, an all-girls school. Unlike my elementary school, where I had friends from the moment I came here, it was much harder. That was partially because of how hard it became for me to connect with people, but also because the girls there were much different in demeanor.

Transitioning from girls to young women wasn't easy for any of us and penetrating any of our armor wasn't easy. Hormones were high and attitudes were strong. For the first time, I started to have run-ins and issues with other girls. The first time I ever got in any real trouble at school was for standing up to Shamika Moody. I'd left my bag on a chair in our classroom that she claimed was hers. When she picked up my bag and tossed it across the floor as far as she could, I returned the fire by doing the same to her.

We didn't throw any punches, but we got in each other's faces and words were exchanged.

Restored

Eventually we allowed the storm to pass between us and became friends. Not only did I gain a girlfriend, but, more importantly, standing up for myself gave me my voice back. My self-imposed silence ended because of that altercation. It was as if a muzzle had been removed from my mouth.

From 7th to 9th grade, I had shoved my pain deep down and I felt like I was coming into my own. I was learning a lot, beginning to become a bit more independent, and I started learning more about the dynamics of catty female relationships. I was involved in the 4-H Club, I loved cooking classes, food & nutrition, clothing, and textiles. Once I learned to sew, I was excited to make my own clothes. That became my favorite new hobby. I made a cute, pleated skirt and vest. As proud as could be, I wore it as often as I could.

I competed in cooking competitions and our school talent shows etc. I was learning to have fun and be a kid again. The transition was difficult.

I wanted to be normal and begin to do the things the other almost-teenagers were doing. I wanted to be normal. I wanted to be fun and free. But I never was, externally I seemed ok. Internally I was miserable. Until I got to high school, I wasn't allowed to pierce my ears and mostly wore my natural hair. Then Dad allowed me to finally wear earrings and perm my hair. Grandmother shared the news with mom in the States and she flipped out. I had finally begun to become comfortable with the person I was becoming. My friend's group grew. Life was good. I was maturing, all while feeling empty inside.

Some people fear death, but I had already died. At least a part of me had. Sexual abuse is one of those experiences that linger in the background of your mind and life. In fact, the worst thing that could ever happen to me had already happened at nine years old. I didn't know that the pain could get worse.

Restored

The level of pain I was about to encounter, I would never see coming.

The Devastation.

By the time I turned 16, I was beginning to bury the hurt I already encountered. But life was about to get worse.

So much of what happened is a blur, blocked from my memory and never to be revisited. The experience comes back to me in bits and pieces—scenes from a horror movie that I never want to see again.

I was in a moving vehicle. People who I had never seen before kept asking if I was okay, but I remained silent, tears rolling down my face as my mind attempted to process what took place. I looked down at my wrist and could feel the stickiness of that tape that once roped my wrist together. My clothes were filthy and ripped into pieces as I tried to stand. I was trying to make sense of it all.

I heard a strong voice behind me yell out, "Washington Blvd!"

I was on a bus. As if waking from a deep sleep, I realized the place was familiar; it was my stop. I stepped toward the door behind a guy in a red shirt and I practically stumbled off the bus, in a haze. Thoughts raced in my head.

What happened this time?

Where had I been taken?

I couldn't piece anything together about what could have happened. I did know one thing as I felt the nervousness and anxiety rise in my chest. I didn't know what time it was, but I knew it was late. And that meant I'd missed my curfew. Fear gripped me, not because of what happened, but because the curfews were something my grandmother took very seriously.

My Grandpa did too. He always said that young ladies shouldn't be outside past a certain time.

Restored

As far as they were concerned, there were no excuses. The rules were the rules.

I came off the bus behind a guy, barefoot and dirty, as if in a trance, I walked through the neighborhood streets. Tears flowed but still the feeling of the man's breath and body lingered in my mind as if I were still there with him.

When I got home, I remember cautiously walking toward the front door. No matter how much my soul had been shattered, what mattered was the fact that I was late for curfew. As I knocked at the door and it opened, I was nearly frozen in place. My grandmother was furious.

I was bruised and tattered. My clothing was ripped. I was visibly dirty. I had been brutally abducted and raped. Surely someone, anyone, could see that something had happened to me.

Did they understand that I almost died that day?

Did they understand that I had to beg and plead for my life that day? After the rape, the rapist asked if I could be his girlfriend. Which maniac does this? But this became my saving grace. I decided then to put on my best show. When he wanted to kill me, I agreed to the promise of being his girlfriend. Because of this, he didn't kill me. This lie saved my life.

Still, as I stood there before my family, and no one seemed to care about what I had endured. Nobody reached to hug me or console me. That was all I wanted and needed at that moment. Hours before, I didn't know if I would be alive. As I lunged my body forward to face my grandmother, she began scolding me for breaking curfew.

Instead of asking what happened, she shouted words forever etched in my memory:

"Go back whey you a come from!"

I walked over the threshold of her home, those words pierced my ears and my heart.

Restored

I turned back to her as I was overcome with unexplainable emotions. I felt gutted, a raw, intense pain in the pit of my stomach.

"I was abducted and was raped!" I shouted these words with all the strength that remained in my body. The only response was silence. Her look of nonbelief as if I was lying spoke volumes! "Tell your father when he comes" she said, I wanted to wake up, but this wasn't a dream. It was now my reality.

I fell to the ground. My body hit the floor as the tears flooded my face. All the strength I had mustered up to walk through that door left me. It was like I was standing center stage, all alone, scarlet letter on my chest with nothing to perform. Even when I made the confessions, no one came to comfort my pain. So, I embraced the floor. I was low.

I wanted so much to be held, so I fell to the floor as I knew the ground was the only steady thing that could hold the weight of my pain.

I could see my cousins staring at me in my periphery. I felt this weird feeling of being on display, but they knew too, that I was in big trouble. I couldn't blame them though; they didn't know how to comfort me.

Grandmother walked away from me and over to the phone and called my dad to tell him I was finally home. She let him know of my tardiness. What felt like just a few minutes later, my dad made it there. He barged in angrily through the door, ready to discipline but as soon as he saw me, I could feel that his emotions began to shift. His anger seemed to dissipate. Without saying a word, he took me outside, put me in his car, and sped off. We drove in dead silence to the police station. We walked in, and I stood in silence while he spoke to the officer at the front desk. I was in a daze. This is not happening.

The next thing I remember is sitting at a small desk.

Restored

A woman was sitting across the table, looking intently at me. My father sat in the chair next to me. Both stared at me.

"Ms. Nelson, are you here? Can you tell us what happened?"

"Huh? Oh, sorry." I said, as if waking up from a trance. I realized I was in the police station. My dad stood next to me, fuming. I could tell he was angry, and helpless. "You said you were walking to a bus stop, and I stopped to look at clothes then what happened?"

I started to cry again. A guy said come with him to see some other pieces and then "They grabbed me, threatened me, and said get in the car. I was crying, begging them to let me go. They took me to a building with stairs. His friend guarded the door.

He put me on a bed I kept begging to let me go, he threatened me, forced me to be quiet and remove my clothes. Then he raped me. I screamed helplessly from pain.

He put his hand over my mouth to stifle my screams as he thrusted in me, he was breathing heavily. My vagina burning and bleeding, but he didn't care.

"I am so sorry," said the officer. Can you tell me where they took you before they grabbed you?"

Everything else went so quickly, more questions, the rape kit, and fear gripped me. I felt so exposed.

Everything I had left was snatched that night as if to separate my soul from my 16-year-old body. Though fully clothed, I felt naked. My virginity, my power, my sanity, all gone. I was now officially nothing!

When I made it back from the police station, as I walked through the door, my grandmother's words still echoed in my mind: "GO BACK WHEY YOU A COME FROM!"

I'm certain that she assumed that I'd been somewhere with a boy, consensually, or hanging out with friends getting into trouble. She saw what she wanted to see.

Restored

A "fast" teenage girl who she'd expected to be promiscuous and disobedient, although I'd never given her a reason to see me that way.

She demanded I go back to a physical place. His house. Their house. The street that she thought I was in, having a good time. I couldn't go back there because that is not where I had been. Deeper than that, I also couldn't go back to the girl that I was before the molestation or the rape.

I came from innocence and purity. I came from love. I came from trust. I came from a heart and imagination that believed, like many girls, that the first time a man touched my body, it would be out of love, a love that we shared. That was where I'd come from. Going back was not so easy. Going back felt impossible.

Her words further shattered those already broken pieces of my heart and soul. I never saw her the same again. The pain I felt numbed me.

I gathered what I could from my fractured dignity and decided to take a shower. Weighted with grandmother's words, I walked past the kitchen. Earlier that day, she'd prepped curry chicken and I saw the knife she'd used laying on the counter. She used that knife religiously during our Sunday dinners. I remember it cut with a sense of exactness. I picked it up and slid into the bathroom without anyone seeing me.

Go back whey you a come from!

Her words confirmed what I had always known. My presence never really mattered. And now in the shower with my knife in tow, I tried to wash away the filth of that night. I scrubbed for what seemed like hours in hopes of washing the dirt and pain away. As tears flooded my eyes and face, my vision became distorted. I hit my head against the shower wall hard as I reached under my towel on the floor for the knife.

Restored

I held the sharpest end tightly against my chest with all my strength. I repeatedly pushed harder and harder, some blood flowed from small incisions while I tried to end what felt like the worst uncontrollable pain. I cried uncontrollably for the fear and shame I had already carried thanks to my molesters, from what felt like lack of family support and weirdness at home.

I had become an anomaly, a blemished fruit, and now thanks to my rapist I wanted to just die.

I couldn't seem to push that knife hard enough! I realized even with the pain, shame, and guilt; I couldn't do it. God would not allow me to do it. I felt a force working against my efforts that night.

I emerged from that shower and was submerged into an even deeper lie—that I was going to be okay. Another part of me died when I was raped. And to cope, a new part of me was born. I began believing a lie, telling myself that I could forget what happened to me.

That I could pretend no one violated me and could have taken my life. That I could run and hide. All of that was a lie. A dangerous one. I lived that lie outwardly, but inside I hid and bottled every emotion. I smiled when I really wanted to die. I went back to my day-to-day life, acting as if nothing changed. No one in my family ever brought it up, no one ever asked how I was doing. To this day it never comes up.

To this day, no one ever has. It's one of my "unspoken talks". It was my burden; I walked with it, carried it, and buried it.

Yet on the outside I pretended I was ok.

I cannot say I know where I was in my mind. I don't know how I moved through the days, through my life, after that happened. I only remember the numbness, the awful gut feeling that wouldn't go away.

Restored

While the police station and the officer questioning me was tough, the rape kit, the pills I was given and that whole humiliating process was debilitating for me, my father's response to what happened to me was crushing. I remember his face and the sadness. For the first and only time in my life, I saw him cry. In the car ride home, dad tried to comfort me, he tried to restore my confidence. He assured me that none of it was my fault, and, feeding the lie, that I would be okay. I know he meant well but it didn't help.

Besides warning me to never speak a word of this to anyone at school, I remember the deafening silence most. Hurt hung in the air and neither of us knew what to say or do with it. As a parent now, I'm not sure what words he could have spoken that day to make it better. I didn't want to bring any attention to my tragedy. I didn't want to wear a scarlet letter for the world to see. I didn't want anyone to know. But I did want to release it in some way.

I now know why, but back then, unbeknownst to my dad, I was already carrying loads of pain. I knew my storage was full. There was no room to store more.

My body had been betrayed. I had become part of this secret society where I went through this horrible initiation process that tortures you for a long time. Sexual trauma controls you. Sexual abuse impacts how you behave and speak.

During larger family functions, many of my other cousins would accuse me of being "stooch"[1]. They believed I acted like I was better than them, but they didn't understand that I was in way more pain than they probably ever experienced.

I didn't intend to be standoffish, I was covering and sheltering myself during my pain as best as I could.

---

[1] A Jamaican word that means haughty or better than

Restored

Many times, that resembled silence and deep contemplation. Much of the time my physical body was there, but my spirit and soul were not.

I grew angrier as a teenager because nobody asked me about the rape. They never once asked, "How are you feeling? How are you dealing with it?" Nothing.

Once my father told me to never speak of it, I knew that meant I needed to move on. The rape happened on a Saturday, and I was at school on Monday morning. Most of that day, I asked for an excuse to go to the restroom. I'd go into the stall and cry my eyes out. My grades and test scores suffered greatly. I longed for some true help.

Though I had a few close friends, I never once uttered a word to them about my abuse. My best friend, Kadian and I have been close since we were three years old. We were born one week apart from each other.

It wasn't until well after I moved to the United States that I revealed the rape to her and my friend Alexia I never wanted to hurt her with my pain.

Back then, the therapy or counseling that I desperately needed wasn't an option. Along with the support from the people I loved, I needed a trained professional to help me to do what they were not equipped to. I needed someone to help me to navigate and validate my feelings. To assure me that my anger, my confusion, my shame was not wrong. To help me to get comfortable with my body again. Instead, I was told, "Oh, you'll be okay." I was anything but okay.

When my dad told me not to say anything, I was surprised and not surprised all at the same time. His silencing me told me that I couldn't even speak to him or anybody else.

Coming from a Christian family, keeping secrets and suppressing emotions were the norm.

Restored

Deep in the church, we were taught to pray and push your way through anything that hurt. My family spent an enormous amount of time at church. We went to service on Tuesday, Wednesday, Some Saturdays, and Sunday. That's what we were supposed to do. Keep showing up. Keep serving. Keep struggling in silence. I accepted that my rape and molestation was a secret that would forever remain silent in my soul. I didn't want to but I did. With such a great cross to bear, I felt alone on an emotional island. But there was still a big part of me that wanted love, specifically a love that I shared with a man. I wanted to learn about love. I wanted to know what that felt like, and although I didn't realize it then, I wanted to know if I *could* be loved despite what happened to me. Months later, I did.

My first love was a Jamaican guy named Chike who was in much pain himself. We were young, but our relationship was beautiful. He was the only one I trusted to hold my pain.

I shared with him the intimate details of all I had experienced. I think because of it, he was delicate with me. Though all our high school friends were becoming sexually active, it was never something he pressured me into. He treated me like a lady. We never left one another's side. Nobody else understood what I was feeling but him.

He allowed me to display my true self. There was a pureness in how he related to me. His level of care gave me great hope about the future. The kind of respect that I received from him I had not received from anyone else, up until then. That was one of the things that made the relationship so special. Connecting with him helped me begin to heal. He was my life. In my mind, he and I were meant to be together forever.

However, things began to change with us. My father abruptly told me that I needed to move to the States with my mother.

Restored

I know his intentions were good, as he had hoped to protect me. But now I'd have to be apart from my love. The rape was my dad's worst nightmare come true. Violence against women was not uncommon in Kingston. We all lived with the possibility. But when I was raped, reality set in for him. I was his daughter, and he wanted to keep me safe. Once he felt that I was no longer safe where I was, he decided that it was time for me to go.

I was 16 and would technically graduate from high school soon. Rather than allowing me to linger after graduation to figure out college etc., my parents devised a plan to move me in the summer so that I could be settled and in school by fall in New York. I was devastated in ways that are indescribable.

Leaving Jamaica, the only home I'd ever known, was like ripping the Band-Aid off a fresh wound. I never imagined living anywhere else. I just wanted out of that house.

That was my home, my life. My boyfriend and close friends were there, it was the only place in my mind at the time where I had some love and some kind of stability. From the moment I touched down on U.S. soil, I hated it. Unlike some of my friends and other family, America was never a place I longed to be. Kingston was my place of comfort. I was a stranger in a foreign land.

I went from being with grandparents, cousins, boyfriend, and friends to living with my mom and stepdad in New York. Being around my mom and stepdad I was comfortable. Him or my dad never made me feel uncomfortable, but any other man did.

To comfort myself, I called my boyfriend in Kingston constantly. My mother's phone bill skyrocketed to nearly $2000 during that first month following my move.

Restored

America was different in every sense of the word. Despite all my emotional turmoil, I still loved school. I was settled in school in Jamaica.

I was on familiar ground, so I knew how to navigate well. Now, I was forced to learn a completely new system with completely new people. I got off to a rocky start. When I arrived, I didn't bring any transcripts with me, so the board of education decided my grade level. My new school in New York didn't recognize and give me many educational credits for most of my high school in Kingston, so I was relegated to remedial classes. Imagine graduating at 16 and then put back in the 10th grade. I was so embarrassed. Once my academic transcripts came in from Kingston, I was transferred to 11th grade.

Everything was different. In Jamaica we wore uniforms during my entire time of schooling. In New York public high school at the time, kids wore whatever they chose. At the start, I hated it.

However, when I started receiving an allowance from my stepdad, I would go shopping to keep up with the latest trends. Soon, high heels became my thing. The first few months, I could barely stand up straight, but soon I was maneuvering like a pro.

I was walking tall on the outside, but I was running short emotionally. I missed my boyfriend and still hadn't dealt with the impact of my trauma. I honestly couldn't process it even if I wanted to.

Unlike some immigrants, the United States was not a place of refuge for me. It was not my "promised land." I soon found that I wasn't safe there either. I had only been there a few weeks when a family friend from the States started to make advances at me. I didn't know what to think, except that somehow this must all be my fault.

Was there an invisible "Please Enter" sign on my forehead? What about me attracted them to me?
Did my spirit wreak of brokenness?

Restored

These were the questions that swirled around in my head. As I had been trained to do, I didn't tell my mom or my stepdad. I just withdrew more and became more and more angry and distant from my family.

I was a typical teenager who rebelled. When mom went right, I'd aim to go left. We argued all the time. She had no idea where much of my anger stemmed from. The abuse I'd endured made me a different person. I wasn't disrespectful or withdrawn for no reason. I had been hurt, physically and emotionally. I'd been uprooted from the only security and stability I'd ever known.

Everything that happened to me occurred without my consent. Whenever I felt forced to do something, anything, that I didn't want to do, I got frustrated and I lashed out.

I remember vividly fighting with my mother about not wanting to attend a family gathering.

She'd spent all day getting ready and dressed to go, while I sat around the house watching television most of the day. I knew mom was leaving, but I had no idea that she would drag me into her plans that day. I was in no way interested. I knew while we weren't the most affectionate family, there would be men—an uncle, a cousin, somebody that wanted to hug me. I wasn't interested. I didn't want to be touched in any way. Even looking at me too hard made me uncomfortable. When Mother realized that I wasn't moving a muscle to get dressed and wasn't interested in seeing my family at all, she couldn't understand why.

She wouldn't let it go. She kept pressing me and pressing me until I exploded.

Without a filter, I screamed at the top of my lungs.

"I WAS RAPED! I WAS TOUCHED! I HATE THEM"
Her mouth gaped wider than I ever saw it. I could see tears begin to well up in her eyes. She didn't know what to say.

Restored

Confused and seemingly shocked, who? when? I didn't reply when she asked, realizing she would get nothing out of me, she walked away. I'm certain my response was far from what she had expected that day. However, I felt backed into a corner that I had to fight my way out of.

Rape leaves you empty, alone, and confused. By that time, I was about 17 and I was trying to find pieces of myself. I felt like I was living more than one life. I was one person for everybody else and someone else at home when I was alone. For my friends I was this fun loving, outgoing, happy person, but there was another side that no one understood. At home, I would barely open my mouth to speak to anyone.

I'd spent most of my life hiding everything that I went through because I did not know who I could trust. Being quiet was the only way that I knew to protect myself.

To be seen was to be heard and to be heard was to be found—by people who could hurt you. I never wanted that to happen again.

Rape strips you of your personhood. Rape changes you. I often had a "attitude" or came across as snappy at times. I didn't mean to be short-tempered, but it was who I had become. I became angry, and it was a deep anger and resentment that I felt in every fiber of my being. The truth that I had been left to deal with all this trauma alone, with no concern or regard for my thoughts or desires, enraged me. When I couldn't allow myself to be sad, I could always be angry. It was a much easier, and often safer, emotion to feel. The depth of the pain I endured hurt so much. Anger was the container in which I subconsciously chose to hold it all.

The effects of my trauma carried into my relationships. When it came to people, I kept somewhat of a distance.

Restored

Trust was far-fetched and a valuable commodity that I didn't share with many people. That distrust that I carried didn't just show up with men, but with everyone in my life. I felt that the best place for me was to be alone. I didn't have the tools then, but now I know that loneliness and distance is the last place that we want to be. I needed my mother. I needed my family. I needed new friends and my boyfriend to love me when I came to the States. I needed people. I needed the strength that only support can provide. But I couldn't tell anyone that. I didn't have the words. Sexual abuse robs its' victims of so many things. The ability to trust and to love, to be vulnerable and open with people, it robs your peace and sanity. People have to now prove themselves worthy and deserving, it is hard. Only when we heal and are restored, will we become willing to allow people in.

It takes work. It takes therapy and tools. It takes time. It takes forgiveness. According to Jeremiah 17:7, it takes God.

I want you to understand something that it took me a while to understand—relationships are a gift. The people who hurt you could have easily taken everything from you, including your ability to love and be intimate with people who love you. What has been taken from you is yours to take back for yourself. The greatest gift that you can give yourself is to heal so that you can share your life with others.

Don't shut yourself off.

Do the work that you need to do to heal so that you can open your heart again. Read Psalms 147:3 when you get a chance.

Restored

LIFE APPLICATION PRINCIPLE:

RELATIONSHIPS ARE THE RAILWAYS TO A RICHER LIFE

How have your relationships been impacted by your trauma? Many of us say "we can do bad by ourselves." When we are hurt or still on our healing journey, we tend to withdraw and isolate to prevent ourselves from being damaged and from damaging others. We often shy away from cultivating new relationships or reviving old ones that we may have distanced ourselves from when we were going through tough times. However, intense isolation can be a pathway to destruction. Authentic relationships are the railways to a richer life.

Restoration Exploration

It doesn't have to happen immediately, but I want you to think about this now. Who can you forgive or reconnect with in order to help build a stronger you? What are some steps to get you to that place?

Reflect on this and write your reflections here.

Restored

Section 3

The Effects
The Impact of It All

The Homecoming Podcast with Dr. Thema Bryant focuses on the impact of mental health issues that affect women and men during their journeys of life.. In episode 16, entitled *Healing Childhood Trauma*, she shares an approach for beginning a healing journey. First, it is significant that you acknowledge that *it* happened. Secondly, it's important to take inventory of how the trauma affected you then and now.

Restored

Lastly, it is critical to make the distinction that what happened to you is not who you are. [2]

While we aren't what happened to us, what happened to us can have a lasting effect. The impact of the debris can impact you in one or two ways: it enables you to grow or forces you to remain stagnant. The latter was a reigning force in my life for a long time. When I look over my life, the greatest impact of the sexual abuse was seen in my relationships with others and with myself. I suffered with a distrust of individuals, fear of living, and losing my voice, all of which played a part in what showed up and for which people.

Eventually, I began to settle into New York as a teenager. My relationship with my boyfriend in Kingston was growing, at least to me. We were doing our best to make our young, long-distance love work.

---

[2] The Homecoming Podcast by Dr. Bryant, episode 16.

Not seeing each other every day was hard, but I still felt a close connection between us. Then suddenly things shifted.

I didn't hear from him for a month. I had no idea what to think. Unable to reach him, I panicked. Had something happened? Was he seriously hurt, and was it because we never had sex? Was he with someone else? Every possible negative scenario ran through my head.

I was returning from school one day, and I saw the alert on my cell phone indicating that I had a voicemail. It was him I called back immediately. I'm not sure why, but I knew something was wrong. His voice was heavy and shaky, but firm.

"Sandy, I love you, but I'm holding you back and because I love you-- I have to let you go!"

Those were words I will never forget. They took what felt like the breath from my body.

Restored

There was no way I was going to allow him to leave me. Not now. Not ever. I tried calling him to discuss the severity of what he meant. I was hoping that this was some emotional decision that could be fixed. I'd never given him any indication that he was holding me back from anything. I was completely committed to him. I didn't understand how he could love me as much as he said he did and then leave me without giving me, or us, a chance. I knew that if we could just talk, we could get past this. I furiously dialed his number as if my life depended on it. But he never answered my calls again.

As the reality of it all set in, I felt the hollowness and emptiness in my stomach that only true heartbreak can bring. I called his mom in tears, she tried consoling me. I hollered and cried uncontrollably that day. I was inconsolable. I felt like committing suicide again, it was difficult to accept that the one person who I thought would always be a part of my life wouldn't be anymore.

My plan was to go and rescue him once my immigration situation was cleared away in the States and bring him there with my family. That day never came.

We spoke again off and on over the years until he disappeared but and he would always say I'll always love you and no one can ever take your place but I'm not good for you. He wouldn't ever tell me why. Years passed and my family in Kingston later told me he showed up twice asking for me. We talked so much when I first came, but over time, those calls lessened, mostly because he had no phone moving all over and the cost.

But I loved him, and he loved me. He was supposed to wait for me, that's what we both said. He couldn't hold on. He became a 'madman.' His mental health was impacted from laced weed I heard he was given, in a way that was devastating.

Restored

He had become homeless and began stealing and because of that developed a criminal record just to survive hence his call to breakup but never told me. Between jail and an asylum, his life never came back together again. I still don't know where he is or if he's still alive. But the way I love him always remained.

With that my hope waned again as my dreams of leaving this life behind and starting a new one with the love of my life were done. Though my parents were separated by the time I was two years old, my grandparents were married 30+ years. My aunts were also married for a good amount of time. Their unions helped me to understand what family meant. However, with my level of brokenness, I didn't have high hopes of a solid relationship. Still, there was a part of me that wanted to keep trying. I wanted true love and all that came with it. It was hard for me to open, to trust, and I'd accepted that it may always be difficult. My boyfriend was my attempt to try.

And now he is gone. I pressed forward, but I was wounded again.

In his book, *What Happened to You?* Dr. Bruce Perry states, "What happened to you as an infant has a profound impact on this capacity to love and be loved."[3] Though I cannot recall much during my infancy, I believe that this same principle applies to any age. Love was a challenge for me. The pain and loss that seemed to be a constant in my life began to break me more and more with each blow.

I was young but life in NYC made me weary. The day-to-day war was taxing. I used public transportation constantly. Going to and from the subway, men would harass me and make sexual advances toward me regularly. I never engaged in full conversation when on the street.

---

[3] Winfrey, Oprah, and Bruce D. Perry. *What Happened to You?: Conversations on Trauma, Resilience, and Healing.* Flatiron Books, 2021, p. 75

Restored

I thanked them for their compliments and then I would go on about my business for the day. Sometimes, the words hurled from their mouths were degrading and downright disappointing.

Already deeply distrustful of men, those interactions were triggering for me. I didn't understand why I wasn't allowed to move through the world without being constantly harassed or with the stress of wondering if I would ever be safe in my own body. Anytime I would go out or when it came to people I knew, I was always braced and prepared for war. I did everything I could to keep everyone at a physical or emotional distance. My hard exterior made my heart impenetrable and love nearly impossible.

Based on what I'd been through, none of that was uncommon or surprising.

Regarding the impact of trauma, author Bessel van der Kolk wrote, "...having been exposed to family violence as a child often makes it difficult to establish stable, trusting relationships as an adult."[4]

He also adds:

> *Trauma, whether it is the result of something done to you or something you yourself have done, almost always makes it difficult to engage in intimate relationships. After you have experienced something so unspeakable, how do you learn to trust yourself or anyone else again? Or, conversely, how can you surrender to an intimate relationship after you have been brutally violated?*[5]

Van der Kolk continues:

> *After trauma the world becomes sharply divided between those who know and those who don't. People who have not shared the traumatic experiences cannot be trusted, because they can't understand it. Sadly, this often includes spouses, children, and co-workers.*[6]

---

[4] Kolk, Van Bessel der, MD. *The Body Keeps the Score: Brain, Mind, and Body in the Healing of Trauma.* Reprint, Penguin Books, 2015, prologue.

[5] Kolk, Van Bessel der, MD. *The Body Keeps the Score: Brain, Mind, and Body in the Healing of Trauma.* Reprint, Penguin Books, 2015, p. 13.

[6] Ibid. p. 18.

Restored

I had a difficult time trusting. I was reserved or emotionally standoffish. I would cut people off quickly and would not think twice about it.

From the time I came to New York at 16 until about 30, the city was hell on earth for me. My body and sexuality seemed to be at the forefront of every interaction I had with a man, stranger or not. I would get weird advances from strange men, which I hated. And I found that my disgust with men wasn't limited to those who catcalled and made offensive and inappropriate comments to me on the street. I was often repulsed by all men. I craved love, but often looked for it in sex. I didn't understand, as a young woman, that love, and sex were two completely different acts. Emotionally, they were sourced from two different places. When you don't trust anyone, love is a place that is impossible to reach, regardless of how much you sleep with them.

Once I started college, my relationships got progressively worse. I lived an entire lie. The first time I had sex after my rape was 5 years later at 21 years old and I regretted it and him. I relived my raped the whole time. I was numb and completely disconnected. I dumped the guy attempted suicide and stopped dating for months. Months later I began craving it again.

Sex was awkward and I trusted no one, so there were no true, lasting connections with men then, only anxious, surface-level attachments. Between 22-24 life was very rough. It was filled with tons of promiscuity and lust. I wanted sex but didn't enjoy it. After intense acts, I wanted it again and I never knew why or how to stop the urge. Yet, I felt used, dirty, and damaged each time.

I never understood why I had these feelings. There were tons of mixed emotions running through me.

Restored

On the one hand, I wanted to be loved and I wanted sex, but on the other hand, often during the act, I just felt like I was raped again and wanted the person to get off me.

I was so confused. I would never reach a climax unless it was oral sex or masturbation. I faked like I enjoyed most of my sexual experiences. I tried finding love and dating in college and attempted to enjoy it. But I always ran or dodged guys.

A portion of the time was pleasurable but much of it I hated. I could never seem to shake the craziness of it all. I felt like an addict. What was done to me I would ask. How can u rape me then now I feel like I can't control my sexual cravings?

It got to a point when my urges for sex for were completely out of control. One of my lowest moments happened, when out of desperation, I let my lust lead and asked a man I'd just recently met to meet me at my house.

He wasn't a complete stranger, but we'd just been introduced and were just starting to get to know one another.

When he got there, we had sex right outside in his car. I didn't care if anyone saw us, including my mother. It was as if sex had this stronghold over me that I couldn't shake. My mind was present, but my spirit wasn't. I just wanted to feel something that wasn't painful. After that happened, I knew I needed some major help. It was at the lowest place I had ever experienced.

What in the hell did I just do? I thought.

I went back into the house and ran to the shower. I scrubbed myself as hard as possibly could. I was 22 at the time, but what I'd done took me back to the sixteen-year-old girl who was raped that night in Kingston again this time I was freaked. I was her all over again. Dirty. Used. Discarded.

Restored

After this sexual encounter, I attempted suicide. I started hitting myself. I was screaming. I was angry. I was there physically but my mind was somewhere else. It was like I was a robot. There was no joy or happiness. Just rage, resentment, and an emptiness that nothing could fill.

Time after time, I subjected myself to dating or talking to men, knowing deep down that every experience would be as horrible as the last. After each dump I did I waited months before I tried it again.

This cycle lasted for almost 2 years—I'd talk to some guys, few I slept with, but most of them I ghosted.

Sex was never completely enjoyable for me, no matter how hard I tried to convince myself otherwise. There was never an emotional connection. There were few true emotional attachments, but I dreaded it. It was mostly only transactional. I felt like a blow-up doll that was just lying there. I was too unhappy to ever have something special with someone.

No matter how many times I did it, there was nothing pleasurable about it during the actual encounter. The thought of sex would make my skin crawl. I hated it.

I also used sex as a means of control and to keep men at bey. The minute I elevated any relationship to some emotional intimacy or sex, I was done with the person. Some of the guys were really nice people. We would have a great time together.

However, once we got to a certain point, I would cut them off almost immediately.

I thought that if I could learn to enjoy sex somehow, that I could feel differently about it. I started to watch porn to teach me about various positions, to gain a level of comfort during the process. I had hoped it would help me become more at ease and confident in bed. I wanted to prove to myself that I could be normal enough to engage at this level of intimacy and enjoy it. None of it helped.

My internal pain was inextricably linked with sex. It made me crazy. It wasn't just the physical aspect that I was struggling with. It was the emotional part of it all. I was looking for something that I never received from my father, at least not consistently. Like most Caribbean men, my dad wasn't affectionate. Deep-down, I yearned for his nurturing.

I looked for that in man after man for a long time. I wanted that affection and affirmation more than anything else.

In the same book, *What Happened To You?*, co-author Oprah Winfrey states, "…if you have experienced trauma but haven't excavated it, the wounded parts of you will affect everything you've managed to build."[7] This is exactly what was happening to me. I tried to build relationships, sexual and otherwise, but they all eventually failed.

---

[7] Ibid. p. 98

I remember being settled in the fact that I didn't need anybody and that I was so broken that my life was not going to change for the better. Fear gripped me to the core. I went to the extent of pretending I never existed. I would come home for the day and sit in the corner so as not to get in the way of anyone else's life. I wanted to disappear.

The fear became fraudulent. For years I pretended that everything was okay. I plastered on the smile, yet there was a big hole that I covered.

It was the one thing in the room you couldn't move. At home, I was a complete mess. I felt unseen. As a kid, I felt like my grandmother always favored my cousins more. As I grew older and entered relationships, I brought that emotional baggage and unhealed wounds right along with me. I convinced myself that people didn't really want me, at least not the real me, and that I was tolerated more than I was loved and wanted.

Restored

I blamed everyone for the pain I experienced. Every experience I had pointed back to the pain of my molestation and finally the rape. I couldn't piece the entire puzzle together then, but I knew enough to know that those past traumas were creating problems in my present life.

At 24 I met a guy 2 years older than me sometime after having to drop full time school because of immigration issues who I thought I could trust. After talking for months, slowly I began letting my guard down and things were seemingly great between us. He came from a solid family and things started fine. He made me believe that my dream of creating a healthy family was finally possible.

Since I was out of school at this point and had no documentation, months later I moved in to help his sister with her baby. We ended up pregnant and we got married. I had left my home and moved in with his family and him.

It felt like I went to bed with a dream—a loving husband, a peaceful home, beautiful children—and woke up to a nightmare after a while. I discovered soon after my husband was having inappropriate conversations with 5 women while I was 3 months pregnant. We weren't even married for a year. Devastated and depressed, I didn't want to bring a child into that situation. My life was now an even bigger mess.

When he betrayed my trust with repeated issues of infidelity not just then but even afterward, along with the continued disrespect, it shattered my world in a way I don't think he realized it would. Though he was the one who cheated, I knew my own brokenness played a big role in us severing ties. Deep down, not only did I want to end it, I wanted him to betray me to prove myself right.

I was sure about the way things would play out.

Restored

It was a cycle—hurt me, cause pain in the relationship, or leave. I never truly believed that my husband was different.

Our verbal arguments were horrendous. Nothing was working. He was not employed at the time we met, but I fell in love with who he was and with the idea of building something together. The more I hoped, the more things worsened. I kept my mouth shut far more than I spoke. I internalized so much of my pain. Those intense feelings from every hurtful experience in my life came upon me again. I became so depressed and did not want to live.

I was 25, married with a kid on the way and had attempted suicide again, as my divorced loomed nearby. It was tough. Though I hollered at the top of my lungs at him when I found out about the affairs, it ultimately shut me down even more. Though he violated the covenant, I placed a lot of blame on myself. I was broken and hurt.

I don't think he understood how deep it ran. I didn't even understand me. I never trusted him again no matter how I tried. I couldn't, instead I resented him. Getting pregnant while caught in my own personal whirlwind was devastating. I was not in the position to effectively care for a child. My child was a product of a marriage that had fallen apart at the seams. Thankfully, God has a way of taking some messed-up situations and creating some amazing things out of it. Out of all that chaos and uncertainty, I received my beautiful daughter.

We were together for three years, but I never revealed to him the extent of my past pain, and I'm not sure he ever once tried to figure it out. He was not ready for marriage, he made some effort but was immature, irresponsible, selfish, and concerned only with his needs. I was done with relationships. Once I made that declaration I was done.

Restored

My marriage had begun to fall apart, and, at the time, we were in the middle of the immigration process that had taken everything from me before we met. See when I got here at 16, my immigration paperwork had issues. My mom had to switch attorneys a couple of times to try to sort it all out. By the time I got into the system, I was already 21.

At that age, the immigration system ages you out, and your parents can't vouch or file for you any longer. This left me stuck between a rock and a hard place. I had to stop college. I was working and going to school, but without money I couldn't pay my tuition. I was no longer in the country legally, so I couldn't apply for financial aid. I lost everything. So, when I met him, I had nothing either. At that point, every pain that I had ever experienced came flooding right back to me. I had no money. No family nearby. No husband that I could trust and rely on.

No safety or the stability that I desperately needed. I felt like I was tolerated and couldn't breathe.

Shortly after giving birth, I was pregnant again. Already struggling with a newborn, and a bad marriage I couldn't handle it, I cried every-day. I didn't want to it hurt so bad, but I decided to abort the baby. This was something he and I had thoroughly discussed although he didn't like it, but we agreed with everything in play financial and otherwise it was the best choice, and he took me. However, the minute he thought it ok to declare I should have been a one-night stand and then throw the abortion in my face when he got caught cheating, that was the moment I knew I wanted nothing to do with him in any sense and that it was the right decision. I didn't see any other way. I couldn't see myself bringing two kids into a lying-cheating-drama of a mess. I wasn't the least bit interested in involving another life in any of it. I wanted out. I cried so much it was ridiculous.

Restored

I was called a gold digger and lied on numerous times by some of his family. No matter what I did it was never enough. I cried more in the marriage than I was ever happy in it. I had met him when he had nothing and loved him as he was broke and living at home but it felt like I was being forced to prove this to everyone else.

I felt alone and trapped within the marriage, at the mercy of him due to immigration. It was the worst feeling ever. We fought constantly. I didn't realize it then, but I was in a deep depression. There was no one to turn to because we don't talk about depression in my culture. So, once again, I was suffering in silence.

I moved back to my mom's home after leaving my ex with my daughter in tow. I was hurting in unimaginable ways. I had to go back to my second home to try to rebuild.

I was livid with his mess, so I became vindictive and since he didn't care about my feelings or stood up to anyone for me I hurt him by setting it up to look like I cheated. I didn't ... but hurt people hurt people. It wasn't the best idea, but I was angry and with men, unless they experience the pain you felt, your level of pain isn't something they understand completely. Ultimately, he told people I left because I was the cheater. I no longer cared about how he damaged my reputation, I just wanted him out of my life. I no longer cared about the relationship. I was tired of being played and lied on and to, and him wasting my time. I felt like I was raising another child that I did not birth. I was done. Handling my child and my immigration issues was now my highest priority. Without citizenship, I felt completely unstable and unsafe. I could not work legally, get an apartment, or do anything to support my child.

Restored

My life and my daughter's life hung in the balance, so I waited on that immigration paperwork to be resubmitted then I left. He got mad when I said I wasn't coming back when he called and one day put my clothes in bags and left them on my mother's steps, he shut down my bank card, life insurance, and cell phone. No matter what he said or how much he called I had enough, so it didn't matter anymore what he did.

Deep down I wanted my marriage to work. I had endured a lot. I held so much pain in and did not speak on certain issues. I heard negative comments people made but I let those stones build me. The truth of the matter is, I loved someone who didn't want to be in a marriage. He didn't know who he was or what he wanted. This proved itself when I realized while separated, he was dating a friend of his dad's daughter before the ink from the divorce was dry.

I no longer cared and although a hard truth pill to swallow I had already made the decision before I left, so, I divorced him. Starting this new chapter of my life was a major turning point. I started to forgive myself. I began to accept that everything that had happened to me, and my response to it, wasn't my fault. I had been a hurt little girl and a wounded woman.

I had endured emotional blows that had knocked me down and almost permanently shattered me. I started to realize I had to deal with myself and all the emotions and pain that I'd buried so deep inside. I felt hurt, anger, and confusion. I knew I needed to heal and couldn't do it around him.

I started getting counseling and began openly communicating more. I began to see that I needed to face a lot of stones in my life that I had left unturned. I started to focus on working on myself, digging up the pain, and connecting what I'd experienced to how I dealt with everything else in my life.

Restored

I began walking down a road towards redemption. I didn't beat myself up as much anymore. I was determined to love and be loved.

Before then, relationships never worked out. My daughter was my first saving grace.

She was my first true experience with how to love someone, outside of myself. Though I loved my parents and grandparents, in our culture we weren't very expressive or affectionate. We didn't tell each other "I love you", kiss, or hug. We didn't talk about our feelings. We didn't discuss relationships much or sex. All of that was new for me.

My daughter opened me up in ways I never thought were possible. She kept me alive and, in many ways, brought me back to life, over and over again.

Though my marriage ended, my life continued. Through the tumultuous marriage, however, I had a gift of another life that I was now responsible for. I deepened my commitment towards her.

Watching her grow, I knew she was a direct blessing from God. Her presence began to change me forever. When things got tough, I rolled up my sleeves further to do whatever needed to be done.

I was determined to provide her the best life I could. I was willing to sacrifice everything for her, and when I was tired, I knew that I couldn't quit. I was working for a construction company and would leave home at 4:30 am to make it to work by 7:30 am. I did whatever I had to do for her. I loved that job.

Almost 2 years later, between working the hardest that I'd ever worked in my life and finishing my Honors Bachelor's degree, I hadn't yet given up on love. During this time, I lost again, this time my best friend that I spent days with since we were 3 years old passed away from lupus. That tore me to shreds. It stung hard but I kept fighting.

So, I made a big change. Due to NYC's high cost of living, I moved to South Carolina to start over.

Restored

While there, I dated someone who eventually truly reminded me that men were full of it. His attitude was atrocious when he was upset and while he believed he was slick, I saw through his ignorant games. To date, it was one of the worst relationships I've ever experienced aside from my marriage (though his parents are amazing). I spent the next 8 months taking care of my kid. Eventually, I decided to try online dating. Almost a later, I met another guy and moved in with my cousin in Atlanta. Despite his advances, I was hesitant to start dating anyone, and I was scared to open my heart completely.

As we talked more, I learned that he worked hard, and he seemed genuine. He was a true gentleman, and respectful in a way I hadn't yet experienced. Sadly, this made me skeptical.

Still, I subconsciously battled the idea of being unfixable. What was wrong with me? Why aren't my relationships lasting?

I still had questions, but, naturally, I still wanted to be loved. I was willing to try. So, we did.

He was a truck driver. The demands of his work required lots of time away from home. The more work that was available, the more he took on. We dated for 6 months and found out we were pregnant. He proposed and we moved in together. However, because of his job we spent far more time apart than we did together.

Almost a year later while planning a wedding, I discovered him cheating with another woman. When I confronted him about his infidelity, his demeanor began to shift. He became vindictive towards me and was willing to hurt our 6-month-old son in the process. When I told him I was leaving the relationship, out of anger he left our son home alone. As I approached the front door that day, I could hear my son's piercing screams from outside.

Restored

Panicked, I ran into the house. I walked towards my son, and I could smell the stench on him before I could even get close. He had defecated all over himself. Snatching him up into my arms, I stormed from room to room, looking for his father, who was nowhere to be found. I couldn't believe that what I was witnessing was true. My son was home alone! Immediately, I called the police screaming. I was livid. When he came back, he said he was downstairs, and my son wasn't alone.

I cussed him clean out and slammed the door. I couldn't afford to get into more drama. Moving in silence is always better. This was the final straw for me emotionally. Another broken relationship that I was unable to comprehend. I couldn't fix this, even if I wanted to. And to be honest, I didn't want to.

My soul was tired. Now a mother of two, I wanted to take my children and go. Still, I didn't leave right away.

I didn't want to go back home to face my family in New York, yet again. Besides, it was too expensive to live there, especially with two young children.

I stayed there until I could put a plot and plan in place. It would be difficult but proved perfect. We avoided each other. He made comments and I operated like he was non-existent. Quietly, I had a police investigation pending after the home alone situation with my son. During that time, I had received death threats sent etc., from him, weird calls and texts trying to scare me. The police detective warned me to tread lightly until I left from around him.

Something in me had shifted. I began to stand up for myself. I refused to ever feel that raging anger that I'd reverted to when I was younger anymore, but I would do anything to protect myself and my children.

I wouldn't hesitate to do what I needed to do. I began to regain my worth, in myself, by myself.

Restored

Eventually I left. I knew that things would only get worse if I didn't. I packed up my kids and moved in with my cousin in Decatur. By the time I left, another woman was pregnant with his child. Departing when I did was the best thing that I could have ever done.

With everything in me, I knew that my children and I deserved better. Still, this relationship was yet another instance of complete and utter failure.

I gained a man-child, my beautiful son, and, for that, I was grateful. He is indeed another one of God's blessings. From each of my broken relationships, I'd gained two children, and, at the same time, lost so much more of myself.

As much as I wanted to blame my children's fathers, I could not hold them completely accountable for my decisions. They were broken too, but I chose them. I was the common factor in all my life's disasters.

What was it about me that kept men cheating?

I pondered this question for years, as any woman would. But I was done.

Then I changed the game. I threw myself into becoming a great mother to my children. I had hoped their fathers would be consistent. One is somewhat consistent now (wasn't always) the other (Mr. King threats) I told to stay gone. . Ultimately, I was a single mother, raising two children as best I could. My first and foremost responsibility was to them.

I also had a responsibility to myself. I saw a pattern and wanted to break it. I learned that when I was hurt, I would look for comfort in relationships that were void of anything meaningful.

I knew that having a healthy loving relationship had as much to do with me as it did with the men that I allowed into my life. I had to figure out how to repair and restore the person who mattered most. This person is the one I face every-day in the mirror. I was ready.

Restored

After ending my relationship and engagement with my son's father, I took an intentional and much-needed break from dating for 3 years. I needed to learn all about myself.

Working and taking care of the kids was a lot, but when time allowed and as they got older, I had to get used to being alone. Instead of running to a relationship when I felt times got tough, I turned to myself. I would take myself to the movies, shows, traveling, shopping, you name it, I did it. I figured out what I liked and what made ME happy. It was the most exhilarating thing I'd ever experienced.

In claiming a stronger sense of self, I also reclaimed my voice. With a strength that I didn't know I had; I grew into a woman that was drastically different. It took time, years even, but I began to start speaking up for myself more and more, I even held leadership positions. That shy, timid girl became a woman who could express herself honestly and purposefully.

The change was noticeable to others around me. Sometimes I wish I had that strength in my twenties. If I had, so much of my life would have been altered. Different woman, different decisions.

I wish I could say that coming into this new sense of strength came without waves of regret and disappointment. Both of those feelings were so real for me, and I spent so much time wrestling them. While I felt so much more empowered to make better decisions for my future, I couldn't completely erase and forget my past. When I thought about the harm that I caused myself emotionally, how much I hurt my body, my heart, and my soul, it cut deep.

Logically, I knew that I couldn't be held accountable for what I didn't know, what I wasn't taught, or for the abuse and its impact. Given time and plenty of therapy, my mind would understand this. It took tons of work to get there and to forgive myself and others.

Restored

At the beginning of this chapter, I talked about the brilliant Dr. Thema and her perspective on how to heal the trauma that we experience as children. She says that to heal, we must acknowledge the trauma, understand how it affected us, and understand that what happened to us is not who we are.

When we are in a cycle of regret and disappointment, we've lost sight that our trauma is not who we are. Once we understand that our trauma happened to us, but doesn't define us, we can look at the trauma and decisions that we've made since those experiences through a different lens.

We can forgive those who hurt us and those who didn't protect us, which is the place in which disappointment stems. We can extend ourselves the grace that we deserve for not knowing what we didn't know, and even for not protecting and defending ourselves.

Some of our trauma was caused by people that we loved and trusted. When that happens, it can leave us mistakenly casting blame on ourselves. We'll blame ourselves for not telling anyone. For not screaming or fighting back. For allowing someone to hurt us again and again. That is where the regret sets in. Disappointment and regret together, is a dangerous dance. Those emotions play on your mind and spirit, and keep you trapped in a cycle of blame and shame. Ultimately, this becomes too heavy of a burden for you to bear. Eventually, I had to learn to live in what I could change and not dwell on what I could not change.

You must do the same.

Your healing work is to release yourself from disappointment and regret that your trauma has left you with. Give yourself the permission to feel that pain and examine all your relationships.

And that includes the one with God.

Restored

We'll talk more about mending your relationship with God in the next chapter but know that your disappointment with God is as natural as your disappointment in the people who hurt you. While your experiences may be different from mine, when you are molested or raped, you will question God, just like I did. I know you've asked, "How could a good God allow such bad things to happen?" I know you've hated the hand that God dealt you at times.

You have a right to be hurt, and trust me, God can handle your disappointment. Ask Him those hard questions. Let Him reveal the purpose behind your pain (believe it or not, there is one). Let Him help you to heal.

If you were like me, you were sitting in that disappointment for so long. Sitting and settling. Settling for being unforgiving. Settling for being unhappy.

Settling for relationships that only compounded your pain as opposed to creating a space for you to heal and be restored. You've made peace with your disappointment, accepting that it was something that you would just have to live with for the rest of your life. But what if I told you that you didn't?

Disappointment does not have to be a permanent part of your life. Neither do relationships that continue to cause you pain. You have relationships that have been broken. You have relationships that are fractured and need to be repaired. How you show up as a daughter, son, a sister, a wife, a husband, a father, a mother, a friend, have all been affected by your abuse.

Every relationship, including the one with God and yourself, will have to be examined. This is the hard, but necessary work required to be fully restored.

Healing is one of the hardest things that you will ever have to do. It is arguably harder than your trauma.

Restored

You didn't have a stay in what happened to you, but you must choose to heal.

As Dr. Thema offers, acknowledge your trauma, understand it, and finally separate yourself from what happened to you.

To do that, you must be willing to face it first.

SANDRIAN NELSON-MOON

LIFE APPLICATION PRINCIPLE:

GRAPPLE WITH REGRET AND DISAPPOINTMENT

It's so much easier to run and to hide from your pain. Easier to remain in your feelings. Easier to not face what is hurtful and hard. Easier to avoid digging up that pain at all costs. However, the cost of that avoidance, that fear, is too high. This regret, disappointment, and hurt that you've been carrying has been weighing you down for far too long.

Disappointment does not define you. Regret cannot restrain you. Face this pain. Grapple with it. Work through it. It will be tough at first. Uncomfortable. Unsettling. Intense. As you look at it head on, things will seem worse before they get better. I know. Keep pressing and grappling with the regret, disappointment, and pain. Your future and freedom are waiting for you on the other side.

Restoration Exploration

Restored

Think about the last issue that you've struggled or grappled with in your own life. Was it in a relationship? Can you see how your trauma was at the root? Can you see how you ran from it rather than running to it to face it?

Consider how you could have handled that differently and explore your thoughts here.

_____
_____
_____
_____
_____
_____
_____
_____
_____
_____
_____
_____
_____
_____
_____
_____

SANDRIAN NELSON-MOON

Restored

Section 4

The Elevation
Healing Forward

It is important to note that no matter how educated, influential, powerful, or articulate we are, we *all* need help. Abuse is a giant that is way too big for any of us to tackle on our own.

Abuse stuns you.

Abuse shames you.

Abuse shatters you.

Abuse leaves you holding the broken pieces of your emotions and life.

Restored

There is no way that you can, or should, attempt to navigate healing and rebuilding yourself without the support of mental health professionals, God and prayer, and other therapeutic tools to help you become whole again.

Therapy.

In my late twenties, I sought therapy. My counselor began to assist me in unraveling the pieces of my life that I had suppressed much of my pain. With her, I became brave enough to face what I feared most. Therapy was the place that allowed me to be honest about every aspect of my abuse. If I am being honest, I came to counseling expecting to lay the blame for every one of my issues at the feet of the men who had abused me.

I wanted someone, my therapist, to join me in hating them and making every negative thing that happened to me since I was molested and raped their fault.

That didn't happen—at least not in the way that I wanted. Yes, they were wrong. Dead wrong. However, in order to heal, I had to give that to God. My healing and therapy were for *me*, no one else. I had to learn how to forgive the people who'd hurt me.

While attending a funeral, I was tested to determine if I was on the right path with my healing and forgiveness journey.

By the time the molestation ended, I knew who had violated me. While at the funeral years later, he came to say hello to me. I was able to respond in peace.

When it was over, I replayed the encounter and noticed that, for the first time, real healing was occurring for me—I wasn't filled with intense emotions like before.

However, I hadn't arrived yet. I still had work to do. There were other people in my life who I was secretly holding accountable for my childhood trauma that I needed to forgive as well.

Restored

Shortly after that funeral where I encountered one of my molesters, my cousin warned me that our grandmother's health was failing. Until then, I didn't realize how much hurt and anger I was holding towards her. When I learned that she was ill and until she passed away, it was extremely difficult for me. I needed to sort out the love from the resentment. Every hurt that she'd caused me came back to my mind and heart. I had to grapple with the favoritism that she showed my cousins and the love I felt she withheld from me.

I recalled her harsh words and not comforting me that night I was raped. All that hurt was still there. To heal, I had to let all that go.

And then there were my parents, particularly my father. I resented him too. I often wondered why dad never thought to take me with him once the rape had transpired. As far I can remember, I did not ask, and it was not offered.

My parents abandoned me in some ways, and, because of that, I felt empty, lost, and confused. As a child, their child, I should have been able to run to them when I was abused. I should have been comfortable and safe enough to speak about anything that ever happened to me. But I wasn't. Not with them or anyone else in my family.

In therapy, I was finally given that space to be heard and validated. I wasn't parented or protected the way I wanted to be, but I learned that I could not carry that forever. The pain was mine to live with.

Yet, I was angry for years at people. Therapy thankfully helped me process some of that pain.

Therapy also taught me that I needed to take accountability for my actions. I was wild. When I think back, it's only by God's grace that I am still here. From the plethora of suicide attempts to the reckless sexual behavior, it's nothing but the grace of a savior that I'm here to tell this story.

If I didn't have the common sense to find a therapist to help me process all my thoughts and emotions, I'm certain I wouldn't be here today.

Therapy helped me to see myself as a woman worthy of forgiving herself, giving herself love and grace, and protection through better decisions. I learned that I could not use my abuse as a crutch anymore. I was not what happened to me. My therapy gave me the lens to see that—finally.

God and Prayer.

Therapy was transformational for me. Still, I needed the grace of God to guide me in my pursuit of peace. There was a void that needed to be filled. I pressed for my children's sake, but I was depleted of my own strength to make things happen for my life. It wasn't a lack of motivation that cornered me, but it was the surrendered posture of my heart. I was done. I was done doing things my way.

I was done making sense of my own life. I needed help. And I had finally concluded that what I needed, no human could give. I needed to separate the pieces of my life to put back together again to make a whole.

God and I had a lot of catching up to do.

Thankfully, He is the patient, merciful, and faithful Father that He is. I'd separated myself from Him. Lost, I was running as far away from Him as I could. Yet, He was right there waiting for me. (Deuteronomy 31:6)

Initially, I was mad at God. I couldn't understand why He'd allowed such horrible things to happen to me. What had I done to deserve that? Why was I the one who'd been molested and raped? Why was I the one that nobody loved enough to respect and to protect? Why do I keep living through this kind of pain?

Why, God?

God accepted my questions and gave me His comfort in response.

Restored

I had to rebuild my faith and belief in God over time. Despite the abuse, God's presence was clear in my life. I'd escaped my rapists. On five different occasions, along with 5 other near death situations, I also reached for a knife and put the sharpest part of the blade against my chest, but I could never push it hard enough for it to penetrate. I'd left not one, but two, broken, abusive relationships with my life and my children, unharmed.

I'd been given the chance to begin again, to live again, and to heal (Deuteronomy 31:8).

God rescued me and gave me the strength to overcome every challenge that I'd ever faced. Through it all, God was there.

I'd grown up Christian, so as I became intentional about growing nearer to God, I felt the familiar feeling of His grace. I had heard the songs, hymns and prayers growing up, but I soon started applying these principles to my own life.

Instead of reciting what I heard, I put the power of my own belief behind those words. I came to God with my own struggles and worship (John 4:24).

I knew Him now in ways that I didn't or couldn't as a child. I could feel my life changing right before my eyes. Prayer became a staple in my life. It was the first place I would go to get refilled when I felt depleted. Coupled with prayer and therapy, I would do constant and consistent reflection and self-adjustments. If I got into a rut, I had to teach myself how to get out.

Through prayer, and bible study I learned the discipline I needed to take control of my emotions. In time, I became much calmer, less angry, and more positive. I finally found a place of peace in my life, according to Philippians 4:7. Check it out.

Glory to God.

Restored

Writing and Creativity.

In healing, I spent a lot of time reading motivational materials. I started getting involved in community work. Those things bought me such peace. I also found myself wandering back to something that I'd always loved—writing. It became my lifeline. I needed to be released.

I've learned that holding the pain in is more damaging than releasing it.

Years later, when I processed my present pain, the weight of the residue of my old pain would come to the surface like an explosion. It often felt like I was pregnant with a child and was prohibited from giving birth. From the time I was 9, I learned about how essential writing was for my soul. The abuse made me write.

In my childhood bedroom that I shared with other cousins; I had a hole in the ceiling right by the closet closest to the window of the room I slept in. There were two queen-sized beds in the room, one for both of them, and one for me and my brother. There was a closet with a hole right above it. I'm not sure how it started, but whenever I felt like writing, I had a cream book with rings on the back that I would pull out, cry and let the words flow. What I couldn't say, I wrote. When I was done, I would hide the book in the hole in the ceiling.

I wouldn't write when my cousins were not around. If I felt the urge to pull the book out, I'd wait until everyone left. If I couldn't put it back in the ceiling, I would put it under the bed. If I heard someone coming before I could get to my spot, I would lift the mattress and put the book in a hidden spot. Then, I would wait for the coast to clear and shove it back up in the ceiling, to its proper place.

Restored

I was sure to not put it too close to the edge so someone could easily discover it. I protected that book with my life. It was my most prized possession.

I can recall times when I would take the book down when I was in high school, just to examine it, write one or two things, and put it back. When I started liking boys, I would write about some of my feelings in it. It was as if I was a walking book of secrets. That's where I started writing, something that I would continue doing for the rest of my life.

As I think back that book was therapy for me. When I couldn't share my feelings with anyone else, I would write it there. I didn't bring that book to the States with me, and to this day, I don't know what happened to it. It was a saving grace for me when I needed it. Later, I transitioned to music for my therapy. And I would get back to singing as well.

Releasing is significant for healing.

I wrote and found solace in music, and both of those outlets were just as powerful, and necessary for me, as my talk therapy. I needed ways to heal my soul, to simmer my anger, and to calm me.

WHEN YOU RESTORE, THE LOVE WILL APPEAR

Love can, and does, heal. All this healing happened because I felt so beat up after all my experiences. Over years the pain kept coming back like a wound that wouldn't heal. Healing happened because I was tired of being that 9-year-old girl trying to escape the midnight violations. I was fed up with reliving the 16-year old's escape of the rape fiasco. The verbal abuse that was a constant companion in my first marriage kept rearing its ugly head in every relationship I had.

I kept wanting to drive a knife through my chest when I got low and depressed. And finally, I got sick of it. I got sick of feeling that feeling.

Restored

Finally, I took a long look at myself and decided that the angry, bitter, frustrated person looking back at me was not the person I wanted to be anymore.

So, after therapy, strengthening my relationship with God, and learning how to make myself happy, I had healed in miraculous ways. After 3 years alone I started to wonder if I was ready to share my life with someone again.

After a divorce, in addition to two other failed serious relationships, it was time for me to make sense of my life. What direction did I need to travel in? Therapy had taken me to a certain place, but I needed to go further. At this point, I was accomplished academically, I had my MBA, had a nice corporate job, a nice home, a car, a business, and I was a great mother.

But there was still something else missing. I needed to explore my heart space. I needed to love and be loved, the right way.

When my daughter was about 8 years old, she saw a TV commercial for a dating service and as she watched with excitement, she exclaimed, "Mommy you need a boyfriend, you need to sign up!" I laughed at her recommendation. Yet deep down inside I knew she too yearned to have a present father.

About a year later, I began to experience an interesting time. God did something different... I ended up in the hospital, near death. I had contracted a very bad sepsis infection in my blood that affected my kidneys and needed to move back to NYC to be close to family. After getting better and settling in, I had another near-death experience.

This time, as I was driving in the car with my young child, and friend. We were rear ended by a pregnant woman while driving on a wet highway. I had to have a total of four major surgeries because of it.

Restored

While in therapy and healing from the car accident and surgeries, a close friend randomly mentioned the same exact site my daughter talked about. After gaining strength, I signed up for an online dating site. When I signed up before, I had no luck. Somehow, I felt it was time to try again.

When the friend mentioned the site, I didn't give it a second thought. I signed up that night. By the time I woke up in the morning, I had already accumulated a few messages in my inbox. Almost immediately, I was overwhelmed by browsing the messages and the back-and-forth process. I tried my best to remain patient. 2 days later, there was one message that stuck out. The man was a true gentleman. His message was brief but very polite. We messaged via chat for two days before I announced that I did not like the site and would be canceling my page. He asked me to call him. I waited a few days before I called him. When I did call, I blocked my number.

Yup, I wasn't playing any games. I quickly learned that he was a quiet, laidback, and a more reserved personality.

This was very different from what I was accustomed to, so I was hesitant but intrigued. Somehow, we talked for about five hours on the phone the first time. I asked a ton of questions. I literally grilled him.

It had been almost 4 years since my last serious relationship. I was ready for a relationship that would work. The more I learned, the more I liked it. We were both single parents and had previous marriages. I was starting this encounter with a new me at a different pace than I had done any others. I waited 6 months before we ever met in person.

We talked everyday but my best friend, realizing how scared I was, asked, "Are you ever going to meet up with him?" I did have plans to meet him, but I wanted to be sure it was right and that I was ready.

Restored

When we finally met, there was a great connection between us. weeks later we decided to hang out in person more. We had fun, we had grown closer as friends, and we enjoyed talking. We then agreed to take it up a notch and went on countless dates and had great conversations and food. Our children however were still off limits for months. About 10 months later we grew more comfortable enough to meet each other's children. We paced ourselves and took our time in every aspect of the relationship. We both understood that marriage took work. We agreed that we'd get it right during the early dating phase or not do it at all. He was damaged from childhood and had lost his kids mom to premature death, and I was divorced and damaged also.

We were both reticent about moving forward in this new space but wanted to give love another attempt. We asked the hard questions early on and became best friends. Do we make sense as a team?

Was this worth doing together? I was very serious and honest about who I was, and what I needed. I was a mother of two beautiful kids that saved my life. He had two sons. And though things were going well, I didn't want my wounds to hinder my parenting, but I did want to become wise because of it.

By this time, I was more confident in who I was. And I was adamant about the bolder, surer woman I had become. I vocalized my needs and desires. In my twenties when I dated there were many men who wanted to rush me into sex.

I finally started standing my ground. I was clear on my standards. I did not want to rush into a sexual relationship. Finally, the power was no longer in someone else's hand. I had become stronger, and therefore wiser. Guess what? The God-sent man I met online eventually became my boyfriend.

Restored

We teamed up, and today we call each other man and wife, we are happily married! As it turned out, we were far more destined to be together than either of us realized.

He was just the person I needed to complete my team. God makes no mistakes, even the thing you think was hell will all work together in God's master plan. Had it not been for the hell, I wouldn't have met him.

God is faithful (1 Corinthians 10:13).

If you take nothing else from this chapter, know that anything is possible. There is nothing that God can't repair and restore. He has given us so many tools—His Word, prayer, therapy, creativity—all of which can help us to facilitate our healing journey. We have no excuses to remain stuck in our pain and brokenness. I hope that, by now, you are grasping that as painful as trauma is, healing can indeed happen.

SANDRIAN NELSON-MOON

LIFE APPLICATION PRINCIPLE:

YOUR WORST POINT CAN BECOME YOUR TURNING POINT

Nothing in your life is wasted. Nothing. Your pain and your journey have a purpose. Whether it was your children, your story to share with others, or breaking cycles in your family, something powerful is resulting from what happened to you. God bought you through your trauma to heal you.

The worst thing that has ever happened to you can be the very thing that God uses to transform your life. Embrace that idea, fully.

Restored

Restoration Exploration

What's been your lowest point and how did that change you? How is it still changing you?

Write your thoughts out here.

_____
_____
_____
_____
_____
_____
_____
_____
_____
_____
_____
_____
_____
_____
_____
_____
_____
_____
_____

Section 5

The Expansion
Growing still…

According to the Merriam-Webster's dictionary, the word "restore" has a few meanings. The one that I love the most is this one: "a bringing back to a former position or condition."

Sexual abuse took away some things. We were robbed of so much. Our innocence, our dignity, and our happiness. Before the abuse, we were little girls, young women, or perhaps more mature adults who believed in people, wholeheartedly. We felt pretty. We felt protected. We trusted ourselves and others.

Restored

We saw sex as something beautiful and special that was to be shared willingly with someone who had our hearts, and then our bodies. We wanted to love and be loved. That is who we were. Then all of that was taken away.

And we never thought that we could get it back.

We were so wrong.

Everything that we lost can be found again. In addition to reclaiming who we were, we can be stronger. Wiser. Whole. Restoration is always possible, through healing. And that healing is a journey, not a destination. We heal for a lifetime.

Because we have a limited amount of time together through this book, it isn't possible for me to share every mile of my journey with you.

As much I want to take you with me into every feeling, doubt, setback, and even success that I experienced along the path I took to heal past my pain, unfortunately, I can't pack it all in here.

I've shared the highlights, the most pivotal moments, and some of the most bitter and sweet moments to paint a picture of possibility for you. Our journeys may be similar, or they could be drastically different. But if you take nothing away from this book, I want you to walk away with this one lesson that I hope you will never forget:

HEALING IS NEVER FINAL, IT'S CONTINUAL.

As humans, we believe that there is an arrival point, a place, a pinnacle that we will all get to at some point in life. We're conditioned to believe that if we do "x" then "y" will always be the result. We're taught to believe that once we've achieved a certain economic status, or have a certain degree, we will have it all together. So, we bring that same mindset to our healing.

Restored

If we've experienced sexual trauma, or any other trauma for that matter, we think that if we do the therapy, learn and practice forgiveness, deepen our relationship with God, and maybe find true love again that we're done with the process. As soon as we can go long lengths of time without battling the depression and anger daily, we expect to never think about or feel the emotions associated with our abuse again.

Until we're triggered and it all comes back.

I am well into my healing journey, but I can't say the memories of the abuse and attacks have disappeared altogether. Those vivid scenes come up at times as I watch my daughter maturing and my son growing up. Having them in the world terrifies me sometimes. It would be easy for my desire to protect them to the point of paranoia. But instead of getting emotionally stuck, I remember, pray, and press forward. I remind myself that my children are safe, and so am I.

For years, every time I experienced heartbreak, or encountered trouble or a misunderstanding in my relationships, it was as if I'd been abused and raped all over again. I would go home and sit in the corner. It's something about that primary pain that becomes your predominant pain. Though the situations and circumstances were different, my emotional response was the same. I had to learn what my triggers were and how to cope with the emotions that flooded me as a result.

Sexual trauma can linger in the background of your life. The thoughts, the fears, and the hurts will be there. The impacts of what happened to you can either break or restore you. You get to decide. It is far from easy, but it is possible to choose to take your life back. To survive this. To still have the life that you desire and deserve.

Healing is your life's work, the work required to have everything that you are entitled to by God.

Restored

From my own experiences, I can promise you that there is purpose in your pain. All experiences provide an opportunity for wisdom. All experiences, no matter how hurtful, are a chance for you to learn and share what you now know. There is always a reason for every season.

Whenever anything is demolished in construction—a building, a sidewalk, a home—it is always resurrected, bigger, better, and stronger than before. Once completed, the new structure is always a sight to behold. Before the abuse, you were happy. You were whole. You were trusting, loving, and free. You will be restored even better again.

Sexual viciousness is incredibly common in our society, and what you feel is much more common that you know.

As indicated by the Centers for Disease Control and Prevention (CDC), about 1 of every 5 ladies in the U.S. are assaulted or explicitly attacked sooner or later in their lives. This frequently happens by somebody they know and trust. In some Asian, African, and Middle Eastern nations, that figure is significantly higher. The CDC goes on to states, "the effect of sexual viciousness goes a long way past any physical wounds. The injury of being assaulted or explicitly ambushed can be shattering, leaving you feeling terrified, embarrassed, and alone or tormented by bad dreams, flashbacks, and other horrendous recollections. The world is no longer safe. You no longer trust others. You no longer trust yourself. You scrutinize your judgment, your sanity and self-worth, and even your mental stability.
You then blame yourself for what occurred or accept that you are now damaged goods." Relationships feel perilous, closeness unimaginable.

Restored

And like other sexual assault survivors, you may battle with PTSD, depression, and anxiety.

I personally experienced almost every one of these effects because of being molested and raped. As I shared throughout this book, after my sexual abuse experiences, I was stifled. I couldn't engage in productive relationships. I couldn't trust effectively. I was full of fear. I was angry. I was negative. I was hurt. I was broken. I was depressed for years and never realized it. I had nothing to give, physically or emotionally, until I began to heal from my trauma.

My healing was not a one and done moment. I didn't wake up one day and forget everything that had ever happened to me. It was a process, a journey, that takes time. I am better than I was twenty years ago. I can share my experiences without being traumatized. I can write these words to you to help you to begin healing and finding your way. I can love. I never thought any of that would be possible.

But when I embraced that I would be on this journey for the rest of my life, God revealed, step by step, what I needed to do next in order to heal myself. He will do the same for you. Start walking.

I'm an apprentice. I'm learning how to live every day. I'm strong, I'm determined. My experiences have defined who I have become and are becoming. I embrace them all because I know that every one of my scars are a witness to His glory. And this wasn't just for me, it was for people connected to me too. God didn't just give the gift of healing to me.

Recently, while speaking to my dad about my trauma advocacy, speaking endeavors and public service work, out of the blue, my dad said something which I could barely hear. I asked him to repeat it.

"I heard you crying in my spirit."
I turned to him. "What?"
My dad further explained, "When you got raped, I heard you crying."

Restored

Those words came from nowhere. I stood there, stunned. My mind went back to that dreaded night. I saw it all again. My dad was standing there in the police station in tears. I had never seen him cry. In fact, the only true emotion I saw I ever witnessed from him was "anger" when me or my brother failed to honor our parents request to curfew. He nearly bawled as I relived the story for the police officers. As I stood there attempting to merge the two worlds: one of being in the police station and the other of being thrown off about his recollection from that night at my sister's wedding. I didn't know what to do. We had never talked about it before now.

The more I share with my dad about what I'm trying to do to impact laws as a future attorney, the more open he is becoming about what he was feeling, what he was experiencing, when I was raped.

Oftentimes, we hoard our pain and our healing to ourselves, but I'm learning more that these experiences don't just impact us. Everyone who loved you is carrying some piece of hurt because of what happened. As you hurt, they hurt. And as you heal, they heal. I had to forgive my father, and he had to forgive himself. God helped us both to do that.

My trauma became my ministry. Being able speak the words, "I was raped," is my ministry. Healing helped me to accept what happened to me, so I could share it. What was once hidden is now out for the world to see and hear. My church knows it. My husband knows it. My children know it. Women and men who know me and who I've never met before, like you, know it. God turned my pain to power for me and so many others. And He can—and will—do the same for you. Lift the shame from the story. Let it begin to heal you. And watch that story transform you and so many others.

Restored

Your journey may look different from mine or some other survivors, but your purpose in God is no different. You're still here for a purpose. You are here to empower others through your story. You are here to still be who you were destined to become.

This is the power of restoration.

You can become who you were—and who you were meant to be.

Before we go, I want to leave you with a few reminders and practices to further help you along your restoration journey: I'll lay them out below:

Sometimes pretending is okay. I know we talked about not suppressing your feelings in an unhealthy way, but as you are healing, you are retraining yourself to live as a whole, healthy person, who may be different for you.

As you rebuild yourself, regain your confidence, and take small steps to live differently, you may have to "trick" your mind and body to believe that you are strong, even if you don't completely feel it or believe it yet. Act as though you already are. Pretend to have it together until you do. Make strong, empowered decisions, even if you are afraid to stand and speak up for yourself. Do it anyway. Eventually, you will be the strong woman that you believe you can be.

Look for reminders. The only reason to look back at your past is for reminders of how far you've come. When I think back to my childhood and the hardest moments of my life, I can't help but to praise God and be so much prouder of the woman that I've become. The fact that you came through your toughest, most painful moments and continue to choose faith over fear every day is proof that you too have come a mighty long way. The fact that you are here is something for you to stand on.

Stand on that, powerfully. And don't allow anyone to tell you or make you think differently.

Make peace a priority. As you are healing, your primary goal is to find and maintain your peace above all else. If you had a broken bone in your leg, that leg could not repair itself if you continued to bang it against a hard surface. Your mind and spirit are the same. You need peace and calm to be able to get well. There is peace available, but we can't find that peace by ourselves. We did not create ourselves. That is God's job. Reconnect to Him. Focus on scriptures and affirmations to help. Rebuild that relationship with God and He will give you the peace that you are seeking.

Find something that does your heart good. Get involved in something you want to do. Find the thing you revel in and do that. It may be writing, singing, or serving others in some type of ministry. Whatever brings you peace and purpose, get into it.

Don't dare do this by yourself. Your pain is too heavy a load to carry by yourself. Get the support you need. Find the therapist, the sister circle, and the ministries that can support you through your healing.

These are the people who can remind you of your strength when you feel weak. When you forget how far you've come, you will have people in your corner who will run through all the ways in which you've overcome and bring them back to your remembrance. We all need people to fortify our faith. Find your people.

These are the people who can remind you of your strength when you feel weak. When you forget how far you've come, you will have people in your corner who will run through all the ways in which you've overcome and bring them back to your remembrance. We all need people to fortify our faith. Find your people.

Restored

LIFE APPLICATION PRINCIPLE:

RECEIVING HELP IS THE HEART OF HUMILITY

I think one of the greatest lessons that one can learn in life is that there are certain circumstances in life that require the wisdom and guidance of others. This may be a surprise to some, but you don't know it all. I have matriculated through some of the finest institutions, and I learned so much. However, there were so many things that a class or textbook could not teach me. I needed God and the people that He put into my life to help me to learn what I didn't know.

We all need help and support. Humility is strength, and with that comes receiving help when you need it most.

Healing is not meant to be done in isolation. Come out of your shell and get the support you need.

I'm rooting for you!

Restoration Exploration

When was the last time you asked for help? Where in your life could you use help, but you are afraid to ask for it? Be honest.

Write down what you need help with and who are the people who are best equipped to support you. If there is no one in your life yet, pray and ask God for that person. And have the faith that they will show up.

Restored

SANDRIAN NELSON-MOON

Restored

SANDRIAN NELSON-MOON

Restored

SANDRIAN NELSON-MOON

www.ingramcontent.com/pod-product-compliance
Lightning Source LLC
Chambersburg PA
CBHW071856160426
43209CB00005B/1071